EVENTS YOU

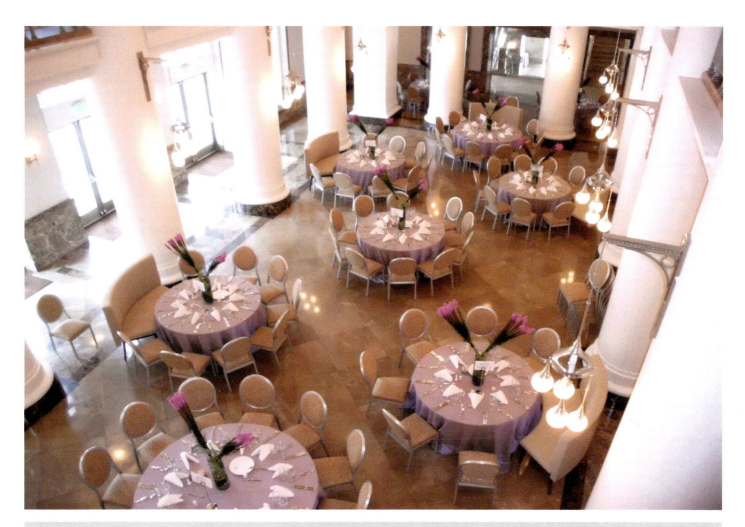

Ultimate Party and Banquet Handbook

TERESA SPEER

TABLE OF CONTENTS

CHART COLOR CODES

Planning	Contracts	Recipes, Menus	Beverages

EVENTS YOU DESIGN
The Ultimate Party and Banquet Handbook
ISBN: 9781466415423
Copyright © 2013 by **BEATLICK PRESS**

Printed by BEATLICK PRESS
45 Garden Park Circle NW
Albuquerque, NM 87107
beatlickpress@yahoo.com

Beatlick Press was established in 2011 to honor the memory of Beatlick Joe Speer of Albuquerque, New Mexico, and to continue his mission to publish deserving talent.

Book design: Pamela Adams Hirst
Printed in the United States of America

This book is dedicated to my late father, Edward Jacobs, who believed in me, edited and threw numerous ideas at me; to my mom, Irene Jacobs, who also believed in me and this project. I want to show my gratitude to my husband, Paul A. Speer, as he worked so hard to edit my book and ensure that the information presented was understandable. Also thanks to Linda Slobey who gave generously of her time, helping me with the placement of photographs, the consistency of content and moral support. Special thanks to the Schermerhorn Symphony Center. It is a true and unique symphony hall. And last but not least, to my editor Pamela Adams Hirst for believing in my project and giving generously of her time.

PREFACE

This book epitomizes thirty years of experience in kitchens, waiting tables, supervision, banquet service, bartending, banquet training, event planning and scheduling of staff. Along the way I garnered many ideas for decorating events both large and small, expensive and inexpensive.

Through my experiences in the industry I have learned how to manage resources, deal with difficult people and organize myself, all very important traits to have in food service. Starting thirty years ago, I spent the first eight years working in kitchens. The last twenty two I have spent working in the front of the house (ballrooms). I have yet to stop loving this business.

Despite the fact I'm not a writer by nature, I still wanted to share my adventures in the food service industry. Then the idea to create a list of decorating ideas struck and I knew from the moment I started writing that I wanted to share my decorating ideas and my knowledge of planning in a book.

My humble beginnings started with my love of cooking. I was always preparing food for my family and friends when I was growing up. My mom, Irene Jacobs, loved the opportunity to take a break from preparing dinner for the family and welcomed my offer to cook on any given night. She was a great cook; in fact, there are recipes from her repertoire that I still try to create to this day.

My dad's mother, Julie Jacobs, was a great cook and influenced me as well. She was Polish and my grandfather, Sidney Jacobs, was Jewish. Grandmother cooked many meals for us, sharing her secrets with me as she prepared her matzo ball soup, barley soup, stuffed cabbages, potato pancakes or potato kugel; just to name a few. I loved spending time with her. She taught me about Polish foods and Jewish cooking. I remember the Polish Bow Ties that she would make and the anticipation of biting into the pastries sprinkled with powdered sugar and piping hot. They were delicious.

This is my Grandmother, Julie Jacobs', recipe for Polish Bow Ties:

CHRUSCIKI BOW TIES POLISH PASTRY

5 cups flour
7 egg yolks
1tsp vanilla
1tsp sugar
½ jigger of Rum or Whiskey
Pinch of salt
½ pint of sour cream
Powdered sugar to garnish

Beat all ingredients together except flour. Place the flour onto a marble surface creating a well in the center of the flour. Pour the mixture into the well in the center of the flour and knead the ingredients together until soft as noodle dough. Cut the dough into 4 small pieces. Roll one piece of the dough to 16 inches by 8 inches. Cut the dough into strips 4 inches long by 2 inches wide. Cut a one inch slit into the middle of each strip of dough, place each end into the slit and pull through. Repeat these steps until all of the dough has been utilized. Heat vegetable oil until hot and then turn the heat to medium temperature and fry the bow ties until lightly browned. Drain them and sprinkle with powdered sugar.

The Campus Inn Hotel in Ann Arbor, Michigan, was my first work site. There I worked in Garde Manger (cold food preparation), prepping foods for two restaurants, room service and banquets. The menu offerings included salmon mousse, chicken galantine, shrimp cocktail, oysters on the half shell and gazpacho; various salads with freshly made dressings; a variety of sandwiches such as the club sandwich; a variety of desserts such as chocolate mousse, chocolate sacher torte and coupe Aruba. Many times I would help prepare foods for banquet functions working with chef Michael Minix.

This chef had passion for his food and taught me a lot about creating stunning food displays. I also learned a lot from the executive chef, Karl Ederle, as he taught me how to create a *mise en place* which translates to the order of things and also sparked my desire to learn everything I could about food. These two men made a huge impact on my career and my desire to cook as a professional, but the need for money is what pulled me into the front of the house.

In those days I served the dinner crowd and on nights where our guests were going to the theater we had to hustle in order to get them fed and out the door in a timely manner. To help round out my experience I worked as a hostess, waitress and supervisor for the dining room of the hotel café. Needless to say that is where I learned that being organized and staying calm was the only way to keep your sanity among the chaos.

Moving from the Campus Inn to Weber's Inn, I did a stint as an apprentice on the hotline preparing breakfast foods as well as various seafood, London broil and other cuts of meat. I spent time preparing foods for off-premises catering to the University of Michigan and ran the satellite kitchen for the lounge of the hotel, preparing a variety of appetizers that would include pizzas that were made fresh daily.

While I worked part-time in hotel kitchens to earn extra money, I was in college studying Food Systems Management. While in college we were required to do an internship at a hospital or other foodservice establishment. I was signed on to apprentice at Haab's restaurant in downtown Ypsilanti, Michigan.

Every week I had to turn in a report to my professor highlighting my week's experience at the restaurant. After completing four years at Eastern Michigan I received a Bachelor of Science from the University and not long after that I moved to Nashville, Tennessee, to be near my brother and his wife and the relatives on my mom's side of the family.

When I moved to Nashville I began my career by working in a restaurant at The Opryland Hotel as a waitress and then hostess. I moved on to banquets at the hotel where we serviced anywhere from two to ten thousand guests. I participated in the training program and worked many of the hotel's VIP functions honing my skills at fine dining.

I also worked in the scheduling office often scheduling anywhere from one to two hundred servers at a given time. I spent twenty years at The Opryland Hotel polishing my talents before moving on to Lowes Vanderbilt for a year and finally the new Schermerhorn Symphony Center in downtown Nashville, Tennessee, where I set up and serve banquet functions and wait tables in the Arpeggio Restaurant.

To this day I still remember my experiences while in college. Back then as now I was a foodie as they call it today. I loved to eat it, shop for it, read about it, talk about it and I loved to cook. I was in love with food and even though I am a vegetarian now I still love food.

When I began to write this book I spent many nights going through notes from previous events I had worked at the Opryland Hotel. This paper work included diagrams, table setups, timelines and other basic information important to the success of the event. I used a notebook to jot down notes of decorations that had been created for events, lighting applications, flower ideas, napkin folds, cake and food displays, almost anything pertaining to ideas for decorating an event.

This is good practice: basically, make a continuing list of decorating ideas and place any pertinent information on party planning in a notebook. My own notebook perfected through all these years has become the basis for this book and thus EVENTS YOU DESIGN has been created.

As I was writing my book I would hand my husband Paul Speer pages to read. The premise was if he understood what I was writing then my readers would too. His knowledge of grammar came in handy. Paul was able to ask the right questions in order to ensure that he understood exactly what information I was trying to convey. He had worked in food service in kitchens for many years and is currently an omelet chef for Bread and Company in the Belle Meade neighborhood of Nashville.

So as you read my book and begin to design your next affair, I hope the planning basics within will help you become organized, the decorating ideas stimulate your creative side while you fashion a blank canvas turning it into a fabulous fete all the while enjoying the planning process as much as I do. If you can conceive it you can create it.

Teresa Speer

INTRODUCTION

"Life is a matter of taste."
Gaius Petronius, judge of elegance

Planning a party can be exciting or stressful. It really is up to you. Follow the simple outline provided in this book and planning will be exciting. There will be no stress and you will create a fabulous party.

The basic steps to event planning enable the reader a simple understanding of what is necessary to create the perfect party. It is important to know how to design a working plan that will enable you to create a successful event. You will learn to plan ahead, budget money, delegate authority, hire qualified vendors and anticipate your guests' needs. The key to your success is in the planning strategies you develop.

The decorating ideas in this book will help you create a unique space that captures your persona. You can create elegance on a large budget as well as a small one. Determine a theme and build upon it with artistic and culinary solutions. This book contains ideas for food displays, bar setups, flowers, furniture, chuppahs, gazebos, tents, backdrops and much more so that you can achieve a unique style for your event. Some of the ideas you can create yourself and some require the help of a professional. It is all about creating the look that you envision.

Why EVENTS YOU DESIGN? Because I hope you will enjoy planning parties as much as I do. After all, half the fun of a party is the planning. You want to enjoy your party and guests. By planning you will enjoy your party as much as your guests do.

Bon Appétit!

EVENTS YOU DESIGN
The Ultimate Party
and Banquet Handbook

Teresa Speer

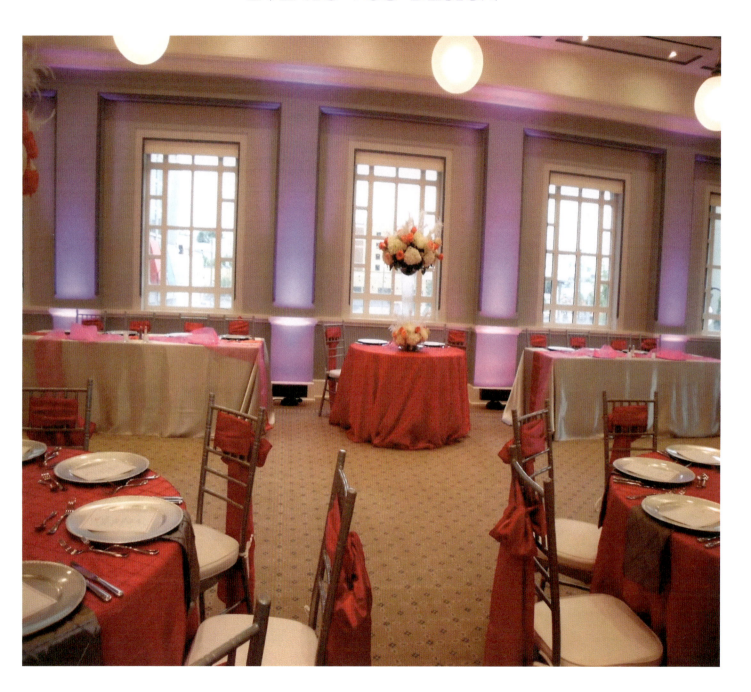

1: BASICS OF DESIGN
Life is a feast. Let the banquet begin.

Planning and Organization

The formula for a successful party is: Planning + Organization = a Successful Party. Planning and organization go hand in hand. One without the other does not seem to work. These are the integral parts to the success of your event. There are many details that must be attended to. You need to set a budget, create a guest list, choose a reception site, interview caterers, create a menu, choose decorating options and decide on entertainment. In order to create a successful event you must design a plan and organize yourself. The information below will help you to create the ultimate party. Remember that the smallest details make the biggest impression on your guests so pay attention to the details.

THE NINE MOST IMPORTANT QUESTIONS TO PLAN YOUR EVENT

They will become the backbone of your event plan.

1. What type of party or event are you designing?
2. How many guests will you invite?
3. When and what time will the party take place?
4. How much money can you afford to spend?
5. What is the most important aspect of your party?
6. Where will the party take place?
7. How will the party be presented?
8. What type of food will you be serving?
9. What types of beverages will you be serving?

These questions comprise the preliminary planning stages and they address the issues necessary to the planning of your event. As you answer each question write your answers in a notebook. Always write down every detail of your party for this is part of the planning process. By planning you will foresee any opportunities that may arise, remember that change is inevitable, but when you plan in advance you allow yourself the luxury of a backup plan.

EVENTS YOU DESIGN

Stay focused; keep a list of everything that needs to be accomplished in order to organize your event. Listing helps you to organize your thoughts. Utilize a notebook to keep all of your inspirations at hand. Peruse through magazines, wedding books, the internet and visit bridal shows if your event is a wedding to find ideas and place these ideas in your notebook. List basic elements such as color scheme, decorations, flowers, food and drink, list your tasks, and check off each one as they become completed. Delegate tasks to individuals who are able to handle them. Jot down notes as you talk with vendors to help as you hire qualified vendors. Do not try to do everything on your own, remember more than one person is involved in the success of your party.

These nine questions need to be answered in order to successfully plan your event. In the following pages I will elaborate on each of these questions. As you read through each one you will have a better understanding of how to answer them as they relate to your party. Take out your notebook and place the answers to these questions in it and you will have the blue print for your event.

1. What type of party or event are you designing?

This is an important question and the first one to be addressed. The objective could be a wedding, birthday or graduation among other things and necessitates planning. Once you have determined the reason for your event you can start planning it.

2. How many guests will you invite?

The next step is to determine the number of guests you wish to invite as this will greatly affect your budget. In order to save money if your budget is tight be sure to tweak your guest list down to an affordable size.

3. When and what time will the party take place?

Selecting an event date and time is an important step in the planning process. If you plan your wedding out of season you will save money. Do not have your event on a holiday unless it is for that holiday, this may greatly effect your guests availability to attend. Consider the time of day as well, this effects the type and amount of food that should be served. It is important to give some consideration to your event date.

4. How much money can you afford to spend?

The next step is to determine your budget and stick with it. Be sure to include every expense in your budget report. Chart 1 on the following page is a sample budget form. Before filling in the blanks be sure to determine the total amount of money you can afford to spend. Be sure to add an extra 10 percent to cover any extras that you might not have planned for originally. Determine the most important aspect of your event as this will most likely be the biggest expense and list the other elements in order of predominance as you determine the amount of money you want to allot to each element. I will discuss this more when we get to question number five which follows this section. Keep in mind that the number of guests in attendance, venue, time of year and the theme will dictate the cost. List those items that you must have and those that you can do without. Be sure to shop around and compare prices of various vendors. This is where the event planner can help. They have connections and know how to help you get the most for your money. Be sure to setup an inventory so that you can keep track of what you need to purchase and what is already available to you. Most importantly you want to stick with your budget so that you are not paying for your event months or even years down the road.

The first column in the budget form lists each element of your event. The second lists the amount you are allocating. The third column gives the actual cost of that element. The budget helps you to keep within the projected amounts allocated. Be flexible as some elements will cost more or maybe less than you initially projected. You may have to take money from one element to make another element happen. Fill in all items that are applicable and add those that are necessary to the success of your event.

SAMPLE BUDGET PLANNING FORM		
Item	Allocated Amount (Estimate)	Actual Cost
Food		
Beverage		
Event Coordinator		
Wait Staff		
Bartender		
Corkage Fees		
Rental Equipment		
Location		
Decorations		
Flowers		
Lighting		
Entertainment		
Wedding Cake		
Wedding Attire		
Photographer		
Valet		
Total		

Chart 1

So far we have completed the first four questions of the nine I listed. The toughest by far to answer is probably question number four. It is not easy to determine a budget when there are so many aspects of a party that can be costly. Renting a location can be extremely expensive. Hiring someone to cater an event does not come cheap. This leads us into question number five.

5. What is the most important aspect of your party?

Determining the most important element of your event will give you a sense of where the larger portion of your money will be spent. It seems to be a consensus among industry professionals that half of your budget will go towards food and beverage. The most important element of your event may not be food or beverage. Maybe entertainment or flowers are most important to you. Determine the importance of each element of your event as this will help to shape your budget. By deciding what the most important element of your event will be and listing all other elements in order of predominance you will be able to allocate the appropriate funds. You could say that the most important aspect of your event directly correlates to how your budget will be determined.

6. Where will the party take place?

Keep in mind the amount of money you have allocated, the distance from the ceremony site if this is a wedding reception and the size of the location in relation to the number of guests invited. Be sure that the location is available on your chosen date. Begin your search and book your location date about nine months in advance. It is not uncommon for a location to be booked several years in advance.

Be sure to inspect the location site to ensure that it has all of the amenities you will need in order to make your party happen. Be specific, look for things such as access to a kitchen, bathrooms, parking and electrical outlets. Know what the hours are that you have booked, if there is a limit to the volume or length of time that music can be played and if liquor is allowed. Find out about deposits, insurance for breakage or bad weather. Review all contracts and be sure to get everything in writing. A contract will protect you as well as the venue that is hosting your party. The contract will ensure that you receive everything that you are paying for. Below is a representation of what might be included on a contract.

INFORMATION TO BE INCLUDED ON A CONTRACT FOR THE LOCATION SITE

1. The venue name.
2. The location of the venue.
3. The phone number.
4. The name of the contact person.
5. The clients name.
6. The date, day and time of the event.
7. Deposit paid or balances due.
8. Cancellation rights.
9. Any restrictions.
10. Equipment provided by the venue.
11. The start and end times for the event.

TIP: For an off-premise event keep in mind zoning, noise and lighting restrictions as they vary from county to county. You may need a permit from the city, county or metro parks commission to set up your event in a public park or beach. Your caterer should be able to assist you with these issues. Be sure to ask the right questions.

TIP: Choose your location wisely, being creative so that you can design a party that is memorable. Prestige, as an example, is not a good reason unless your budget allows for it. You will make sacrifices for food, beverage, decorations and entertainment. Stay within your budget by choosing to house your reception at the church where your ceremony will be performed, sometimes a clubhouse in a private neighborhood is a good choice, you will pay a deposit, which will be returned as long as there is no damage to the property and it is left clean, If you have enough space in your backyard set up your event there. You might find a banquet hall that will fit your needs and if you schedule your event off season or on a Sunday night they will give you a discounted rate.

IDEAS FOR LOCATIONS

There are many unique and interesting options for housing your party. Research the area you live in to find unique options. Look at more than one choice and compare prices and services offered. Choose an unusual environment to create intimate spaces for impressive parties. Below is a list of locations to inspire you while you search for a venue that is perfect.

1. Penthouse suite at a resort hotel.
2. Penthouse suite with a city view.
3. Banquet hall at a resort hotel.
4. Pool side at a resort hotel.
5. City run park such as Centennial Park (Parthenon) Nashville, Tennessee.
6. A library with interesting architecture and space to house an event.
7. Your own back yard with plenty of space to set up a tent.
8. Your house.
9. A lake side view complete with a tent to house your guests in case of unexpected rain.
10. An art gallery is an intriguing location.
11. A banquet facility outside of a hotel.
12. Rent an antebellum mansion where the botanical gardens make for a romantic wedding ceremony.
13. A location with interesting architecture such as the War Memorial Building in Nashville. The majestic columns that surround the outdoor patio and gardens are stunning.
14. A stylish restaurant where you can allow guests to order off the menu.
15. A hotel that has a revolving restaurant crowning its top.
16. A location, like the Schermerhorn Symphony Center in Nashville with stunning spaces and views for equally stunning parties.

17. An old factory like The Factory in historic Franklin, Tennessee, is charming.
18. Choose an historic hotel such as Union Station or the Hermitage Hotel in Nashville.
19. The General Jackson Showboat at Gaylord Resort and Convention Center.
20. A green house is full of vibrancy and life and a great location for a reception or small dinner.
21. The Grand Ole Opry in Nashville is available for parties.
22. Disney world can plan a custom destination wedding.
23. Host a destination wedding in Spain, Germany or Prague complete with fairy tale castles and stunning landscapes.
24. A winery.
25. A garden complete with pond and bridge to stage a wedding ceremony.
26. A wedding at sea.
27. Rent a yacht.
28. A bed and breakfast.
29. A private estate.
30. A terrace overlooking the ocean.
31. A roof top patio with stunning views of the city.
32. A resort hotel with an atrium.
33. The Country Music Hall of Fame in Nashville has event space.
34. A college campus has facilities for events.
35. Rent the hall at a church and have the ceremony and reception all in one location.
36. The community center offers space.
37. A movie theater offers rental space for events.
38. An auditorium could be equipped with a tent to hide concrete walls and floors. House a magnificent party inside the tent.
39. A club house.
40. A waterfront such as a beach or lake front.
41. Rent patio space that has gardens and a fountain as well.
42. A pier that extends out into the ocean is a romantic locale for a ceremony.
43. A room that has windows with a stunning view is always a perfect location.
44. An observatory offers a unique setting.
45. A museum.
46. For a great location choose an aquarium

We have only three questions left to answer and we will have completed the backbone of our event. Keep in mind that it will take more than a few minutes or an hour to answer these questions. You will even change your mind numerous times before you make any final decisions. Questions seven, eight and nine involve food and beverage. A party just isn't a party without them. We will start with presentation which is addressed in question number seven.

7. How will the party be presented?

Simply stated will it be a buffet, sit-down dinner, butler passed hors d'oeuvres or stand up reception? A breakfast, brunch, lunch or dinner? The time of day, number of guests, type of party and budget all play a part in this decision. We will discuss these options in more detail when we get to food in the decorating section of the book.

8. What type of food will you be serving?

Will you offer Italian specialties, picnic foods such as hot dogs and hamburgers, a steak dinner, an assortment of appetizers or cake and punch? The information listed in the decorating section under food will help you in choosing your menu.

9. What type of beverages will you be serving?

Will you have a full-service bar, satellite bar, butler passed beer and wine or a specialty drink as your offering? Your budget as well as the type of group attending your event will help to determine whether or not you will serve alcohol. Read the information listed in the decorating section of the book under beverages for more details on beverage selection.

The previous pages give you a very simple working plan to use when designing your next bash. However, there are several other details that must be attended to in order to finish the planning stages. You need to choose a rental company, and as we discussed in question number four on budgeting, inventory is important and we will be discussing it in the following pages. You must hire a caterer and if you choose to do so an event planner. The following pages have information to help you with this. You must also create a timeline for the setup of your event and for the order of service and these are also discussed in the following pages. Last but not least I have listed some important issues pertaining to party etiquette and room setup and these topics are discussed in the following pages as well. Use these guidelines to help you create the ultimate event.

RENTAL COMPANIES

It is important to choose the right rental company. If you are working with an event planner or caterer they have connections and can help you save money. If not check with more than one rental company to determine who will better meet your needs. When you have your event at a hotel the caterer on staff will help you with your choices. The hotel often times has equipment to suit your needs. Many hotels have a selection of linens and chairs as well as tables, a selection of china and glassware. They are able to meet all of your equipment needs. As you choose vendors such as rental companies make a list of likes and dislikes so that you can compare services offered by each one and rate each item in order to determine which company will best suit your needs. Utilize Chart 6, page 22, as a guide. Take the following list of questions with you as you interview and the chart that follows is a representation of what might be included on the contract. The next section has some basic information on inventory.

SAMPLE QUESTIONS FOR VENDORS
1. What is the extent of your rental items?
2. Do you offer any discounts on bulk rentals?
3. Do I need to make a deposit?
4. How far in advance do I need to place my order?
5. How far in advance do I need to make any cancellations?
6. Do you offer insurance to cover any damage that may occur?
7. Is there a charge for delivery or pickup of rental items?

INFORMATION TO BE INCLUDED ON A CONTRACT FOR A RENTAL COMPANY
1. The company name, address and phone number.
2. The client name.
3. The date of the event.
4. The time of the event.
5. The event location.
6. Deposits made.
7. Balance due.
8. Cancellation policy.
9. Itemized list.
10. Insurance as it pertains to lost or damaged items. Damage waiver (wear and tear).
11. Delivery and return times.
!2. The vendor's signature.
13. The client's signature.

INVENTORY

As we discussed in the section on budgeting an inventory is a very important part of the planning process. Once your budget is complete you want to create an inventory. The inventory that follows, Chart 2, illustrates the need to separate inventory into two categories, one for the assets available, the other for equipment to be rented or bought. By creating an inventory you can see what items you already have and what items will need to be purchased. Items already available to you will save you money.

Make a list of the assets available to you and the assets to be bought. Once you determine what you need to purchase, check with rental companies to see what is available. If you are working with an off-premise caterer be sure to make a list of all of the equipment you will be responsible for obtaining such as tables for a buffet or chaffing dishes.

Chart 2 that follows is a sample inventory. Use it when you plan your events to keep track of the assets available to you and the equipment you need to rent or buy. Your list should include all items to be provided by the caterer and any other items such as tables, chairs, linen, centerpieces and candles necessary to the setup and decorating of the event. The assets available lists the items the caterer will provide and any items available at the facility where the event will take place. The second list has all items to rent and or buy. By setting up an inventory you will know what equipment is available to you and what equipment you will have to purchase or rent. The caterer will inform you of what equipment needs they may have.

If equipment is available to the caterer it is assets available. If the caterer cannot provide chaffing dishes, for example, then they are considered equipment to rent or buy. Keeping inventory is part of being organized. It will ensure that you have all of the equipment needed to make your party successful.

INVENTORY	
ASSETS AVAILABLE	**EQUIPMENT TO RENT OR BUY**

Chart 2

Check with several companies for prices and selection on rental items. Ask questions just as you would when interviewing other vendors to ensure that you receive the best products and services available. Be sure you receive a contract.

HOW TO HIRE AN EVENT PLANNER

Although this chapter of my book is designed to help you plan your event, you may be reading it only to familiarize yourself with the planning basics. Perhaps you are reading this book because you want ideas for decorating and would rather hire a professional event planner to do the leg work for you. This is OK, too. The event planner is the architect who lays down the blueprint that everyone will follow. The purpose of an event planner is to take their client's ideas, visualize, design, construct and produce an event from the client's images, creating the perfect environment. The event planner is one part of the equation working alongside vendors, an off-premise caterer or hotel caterer, chef and wait staff to set the perfect mood, paying attention to details that make your party special while creating an environment that reflects your taste.

Depending on the size of the job and budget you will profit from hiring an event planner. There are benefits to working with professionals. They can create the look that you want and ensure that the day of your event is stress free as well as plan budgets, procure audio/visual services, locate a venue, manage guests lists, create decorations, hire a florist and pastry chef, arrange hotel rooms for out-of-town guests and so much more. Create a list of all responsibilities that you want the event planner to handle to guarantee these issues will be taken care of. To ensure that the event planner is good ask lots of questions, look at references and view credentials. Below is a list of sample questions for the event planner.

SAMPLE QUESTIONS FOR THE EVENT PLANNER

When you interview an event planner take a list of questions along with you to help ensure that their vision is aligned with yours.
1. **Ask to see credentials.**
2. **Ask to view pictures of previous jobs.**
3. **Ask for references that you can contact.**
4. **Ask what services the event planner offers.**
5. **Find out how the event planner handles opportunities that may arise. Having a back up plan is very important.**
6. **Find out if the event planner has contact with vendors that will offer you a discount on any of their rental services.**
7. **Ask if he or she can recommend a caterer.**
8. **Find out if the event planner will help you determine the perfect location for your event.**
9. **Find out how they charge for their services. Do they bill by the hour, the event or charge a percentage of the total budget?**
10. **Ask if you can visit an event as it takes place.**
11. **Be sure that the event planner has experience by inquiring as to how many parties he or she has handled and what size.**

The cost of hiring an event planner will vary depending on location, the size of your party, their reputation and experience. Some event planners have a fee for a basic package. The fee may be based on a percentage of the gross budget or hourly rate. You will pay for time and any extra services provided. Keep track of the prices that various event planners charge and the services that they offer so that you can compare when making a final decision. You will be charged for last minute changes.

Be sure to retain prices and any other information pertinent to your event when you talk to photographers and entertainers as well. You want to receive the best possible deal by negotiating with the professionals. Due to inflation and other factors, costs may rise. This is important when discussing the price of the catered event months in advance. The signed contracts should specify whether or not there are any inflation price increases or if the price is fixed.

INFORMATION TO BE INCLUDED ON AN EVENT COORDINATOR CONTRACT

1. **The company name, address and phone number.**
2. **The name of the event site.**
3. **The address and phone number of the event site.**
4. **The type of event.**
5. **The day and date of the event.**
6. **The start and end times for the event.**
7. **Fee for the event planner.**
8. **Deposits paid or balances due.**
9. **Any special provisions by the event planner.**
10. **The date and signature of the client and the event planner.**

You will be glad you hired an event planner to help with your party since there will be many details that you will have to attend to. Any event of a large size, whether a wedding, anniversary or graduation, will benefit from the expertise of an event planner. They will help you with your budget, direct you towards vendors that will provide you with the services that best fit your needs and be available on the day of your event to ensure that the setup and order of service go according to plan. Sometimes they can acquire equipment and people at reduced costs. The event planner will help to make your party fabulous and stress free.

TIP: Communication is very important. You will suffer consequences if you fail to communicate with everyone involved in the creation of your party.

HOW TO HIRE A CATERER

Before you hire a caterer create the concept for your event by listing any ideas for food, beverage, decorative elements and include your budget as well. A good caterer can work with your budget, but you must also be flexible. Hopefully you have already determined your location site so that the caterer you choose can view the kitchen facilities and dining area. Be sure to put together a list of questions to ensure you receive all of the necessary information to help you make your final choice. I have created a sample list of questions below. Create a chart to help you keep track of any information you receive from perspective caterers, such as Chart 3 which follows the sample list of questions, and utilize it when you do your interviews. You do not want to go overboard trying to keep up with too much information so be sure to interview three, but no more than five caterers. Be organized, have your list and chart in hand when you interview caterers and take notes about each one including your likes or dislikes.

<u>**SAMPLE QUESTIONS FOR THE CATERER**</u>
Do not be afraid to ask as many questions as you feel are necessary in order to help you make the right choice. Knowing what to ask is important. Add any questions to this list that you feel are pertinent to the success of your event.

1. This is my menu. What is the cost per person?
2. What can you tell me about the presentation of the food?
3. What will the portion sizes of the food be?
4. May I see pictures of your work?
5. Do you have food samples for me to try?
6. If this is a buffet; how will you handle replenishment?
7. If I have a buffet will you have staff to maintain the buffet?
8. How much will you charge for a wedding cake?
9. How much for the groom's cake?
10. Is there a charge for cutting the wedding cake?
11. How much will it cost to serve alcoholic beverages?
12. How do you charge for punch?
13. Do you have wait staff available?
14. How many waiters will I need for the number of guests invited?
15. What about bartenders?
16. Do you have staff available to pour wine if applicable?
17. What will the staff attire be?
18. What time will you and your staff arrive to set up the function?
19. Do you have staff to set up tables and chairs and place linen?
20. What about staff to clean up?
21. Will you provide a certain number of manpower hours?
22. After a certain period of time are there charges for overtime?

23. Are gratuities included?
24. Can you present me with references that I might contact?
25. By what date do you need a guarantee?
26. Could you recommend the name of a rental company?
27. Does this company give you a discount?
28. What about a company that rents linen?
29. What equipment do you provide?
30. Do you have chaffing dishes for any hot food items on the buffet?
31. Do you supply china and glassware?
32. Is each item that you will provide and all chargeable costs present in the contract?
33. Will there be an on site contact?
34. Do we need to pay a deposit?
35. By what date must we pay the balance?
36. Do you offer a cancellation policy?

COMPANY	PACKAGE OFFERED	COST OF PACKAGE	LIKES	DISLIKES

Chart 3

When you inform the caterer of how much money you can afford to spend you will be given a choice of food options. A good caterer will work with your budget. The number of guests in attendance, the number of courses or food items served, the cost of the ingredients, how the food is presented (buffet or sit-down), equipment rentals and taxes and gratuities are all relevant to the total bill. The more open to adjustments you are the easier it will be for your caterer to work within the confines of your budget.

The caterer normally provides food, beverages and staff to prepare and serve the food at your event, but you may want to consider providing your own liquor. Sometimes you can get better prices on liquor by purchasing it from a liquor warehouse.

Do not wait until the last minute to hire a caterer or the caterer of your choice may already be booked or charge more for their services because you are at a disadvantage. Start your search at least nine months in advance.

Be sure to ask for a menu tasting. If you are spending copious amounts of money on food you definitely want a menu tasting. Remember, the closer you are to the date of your event, the better you will remember how the food tastes so book your tasting then. If your caterer does not offer a tasting you might pay the caterer to set up a test meal for you and your fiancée and make a night of it.
If you can afford to do so it is a nice gesture to serve the band, DJ, photographer or other help a meal.

You can always set up a buffet, serve a plated option that is less expensive than the one served to your guests or order box lunches, allowing your staff to choose an option that suits their tastes.

Previously we discussed hiring an off-premise caterer, but if you choose to have your event at a hotel you will work with the venue's caterer. Venues such as a banquet hall also have a caterer on hand to help you plan the food and beverage for your event. The venue's caterer will book the appropriate event space, help in the planning of a menu, set up a test meal so that the you can meet with the chef to determine what food you would like to serve at your event and will also book guests' rooms if applicable. They can help when choosing a florist, linen, decorations and entertainment.

From inception to completion you meet with the venue caterer, tour the facility, view the banquet rooms to determine which room will meet your needs and once you have made your decision the caterer will confirm the availability of the room. The caterer will set up a test meal to assist you in determining the menu and all beverage needs and draw up a contract stipulating any agreements between you and the hotel. So be certain to read the contract to ensure that it is correct and that you are aware of any fees or unpaid balances and terms that you will be responsible for. Once you sign the contract the hotel caterer begins the planning process.

Have your caterer put all of the details in writing. A contract is very important ensuring that you receive everything that you have ordered and pricing is what you and the caterer initially agreed upon. The contract protects you as well as the caterer and once signed is a legally binding contract. Both parties must keep their part of the agreement.

CONTRACT INFORMATION TO BE PROVIDED BY AN OFF-PREMISE CATERER

1. Company name, address and phone number.
2. The day and date of the event.
3. Type of event.
4. The time of the event.
5. The name and address of the event site.
6. The number of guests to feed.
7. Food items ordered.
8. Beverages ordered.
9. Any special meals to be provided such as vegetarian or lactose free.
10. The time of food and beverage service.
11. The name of the caterer or on-site contact person.
12. How many servers or bartenders will work the function.
13. Any linen or other equipment that the caterer will supply.
14. Any special information pertinent to the success of your event.
15. Payment information and balances due.
16. Any special provisions provided by the caterer.
17. Insurance information provided by the caterer.
18. The date and signature of the client and the caterer.

TIMELINE FOR THE SETUP OF THE EVENT AND FOR THE ORDER OF SERVICE

The big day has arrived. You want your event to go off without any hitches and it will if you are organized. You have planned your event, but there are just a few more things to do in order to ensure your party will be a successful one. You need to set up a timeline for the setup of your event and for the order of service. These lists are one more piece of the organizational puzzle and will make the difference between a smoothly running party and one that is full of chaos.

TIMELINE FOR THE SET-UP

The timeline is an outline that gives everyone involved in the setup the specific times in which each task required is to be completed. Each task is to be checked off when it is completed. Be sure to give everyone involved a copy of this list. Remember this is just a tentative list and changes could occur. Having a timeline will keep you organized. As you start to accomplish the tasks on this list you will see your event come together.

EVENTS YOU DESIGN

TIME	JOB ASSIGNMENT	JOB COMPLETED

Chart 4

PLANNING IS THE SINGLE MOST IMPORTANT THING THAT YOU WILL DO TO MAKE YOUR PARTY A SUCCESSFUL EVENT.

TIMELINE FOR THE ORDER OF SERVICE

The timeline for the order of service ensures that everyone involved knows the scheduled order of events. Hopefully your order of service will go according to schedule but you must be prepared for change. If this is a wedding, the ceremony could start late due to some unforeseen circumstance. The father of the bride might make a speech that is longer than expected. The photographer may take more time with pictures of the wedding party than expected. Just remember to be open for change. Be sure that each individual involved in the production of your function has a copy of the timeline. This will ensure that everyone involved will be well informed and better able to perform their assigned tasks.

TIME	SERVICE

Chart 5

TIP: Always have a contingency plan for an out-of-doors event. Never assume that the weather will cooperate as it may not and this could put you and your guests' safety at risk.

According to encyclopedia.com, Athenaeus, 200 B.C.E., was a Greek writer. His anthological work, the Deipnosophistae (Banquet of the Sophists), is a collection of anecdotes and excerpts from ancient writers whose works are otherwise lost. According to Google a word beloved of toastmasters, "deipnosophist" is a master of the art of dinner table conversation.

PARTY

In the world of parties there are some socially acceptable manners that you should follow when planning your event. I have put together a list of these practices for you to use as a guideline for making your next event a successful one.

1. One of the most important things you will do when planning your event is to tuck an RSVP into your invitation. The numbers you receive as your guests respond to the conformation card will help you to determine how much food and beverage you will need to accommodate the number of guests in attendance. Remember proper wording on your invitation is important.

2. When you send out your invitations you want to inform your guests of the food arrangements. This lets your guests know if you intend on serving a full meal, appetizers or punch and cake. Your guests may need to eat a meal before attending your event if he or she is diabetic or they may have young children that need to eat before attending your event. Also the guest may be vegetarian or have a specific food allergy and will be able to inform you in advance when they return your RSVP.

3. Place a map with directions to the wedding ceremony site and the reception site in your invitation.

4. When planning a sit-down dinner for your event be sure to have at least two to four vegetarian plates for every 100 guests.

5. During a sit-down dinner be sure to have the wait staff scenario your guests. This allows the guest to identify themselves if they have any special dietary needs. Never allow your wait staff to advertise a vegetarian or substitute meal when they scenario your guests. The idea of the scenario is to inform the guests of the menu and allow any guest that may be vegetarian or have allergies to foods such as nuts or dairy products to be identified. We call the vegetarian plate "A Silent Vegetarian," this option is available to those who identify themselves as a vegetarian and not to guests who simply do not care for your entrée choice.

6. Always have your wait staff assist the guests with the placement of the napkins in the lap before dinner service.

7. Whenever possible introduce guests to one another.

8. Remember to announce dinner fifteen minutes early. It will take a certain amount of time to move guests into the dining area from the reception area for seating as most people are in conversation with one another or they may want to return to the bar for another drink.

9. Be sure to have a reception before a sit-down dinner. Serve cocktails and appetizers to guests upon arrival at your event location so that guests can mix and mingle before they sit down for dinner.

10. When making a speech before dinner be sure to include any guests that have traveled any distances in your speech.

11. If your event is between the hours of five-nine PM you need to serve your guests heavier foods.

ETIQUETTE

12. At a buffet dinner, be sure to have your wait staff assist any elderly guests that are in line, prepare and carry their plate back to their table.

13. It is not necessary to tip, but it is always nice to do so if the staff that works your function does a good job for you.

14. Be sure to make arrangements for those guests that have had too many drinks. Always keep the phone number of a cab company on hand. It is your responsibility to keep the safety of your guests and those drivers that are on the road in the fore front of your mind.

15. At a wedding reception have your staff put together plates of food for the bride and groom to nibble on at a later time. They may want the food delivered to their hotel room if the event is at the same location. Another way of serving the bride and groom is to place their meals into to-go containers so that they can take food with them as they depart the reception. Many times the bride and groom are visiting with their guests or enjoying the dancing and other activities that go along with a wedding reception such as cake cutting, flower toss or garter toss and do not take time to sit down and enjoy their meal. At some wedding receptions the bride and groom have actually eaten their meals in a secluded room by themselves and then joined the party afterwards. Remember to always take care of the bride and groom first.

16. Remember that no detail is too small and these details make a difference in the overall look of your party.

17. Be sure to utilize either plastic ware or china. Never mix one with the other, this will diminish the overall look of your table setting or buffet.

18. Be sure any equipment that will be utilized for your event is clean. Spotted or dirty equipment such as chaffing dishes take away from the polished look of your event and conveys a message that you are not a good house keeper and are not sanitary.

19. If you are planning a wedding reception be sure that the bride approves all linen or other decorations to be utilized in carrying out the theme of the wedding. Never take it upon yourself to use linen of various colors other than white unless specified by the bride. The same goes for flowers. The bride will inform you of her wishes. You want to ensure that the color of linen and the type of flowers match what the bride's florist or event coordinator has supplied for the event.

20. If you have many guests traveling from out of state plan to have a brunch the morning after your party. This is a nice gesture and allows you and your guests a chance to visit as well as feed your guests a much appreciated light meal before they begin their journey home.

21. Be sure to have nonalcoholic beverages available for those guests who do not drink alcohol.

22. If possible have a meal for the musicians, photographers, band and waiters, during the course of your function.

23. Never skimp on staff. You want your guests to receive the best possible service. The next chart gives you a guideline to help you understand the amount of staff you may need for your event. When you have your event at a hotel they will staff it accordingly. If you hire a caterer check with the caterer to see if he or she will use the numbers in Chart 6 when planning staff for your event.

RATIO CHART OF SERVERS PER GUEST	
Type of Event	**Number of Servers**
Buffet Dinner	One server per 100 guests per buffet. Plus one server per 40 or 50 guests for table service. One server per bar. One bar per 200 people.
Sit-down Dinner	One server per 20 guests or two servers per 40 or 50 guests.
Reception	One server per 100 guests. Plus one bartender if applicable.
Reception with Action Stations **Chart 6**	One server per 100 guests plus adequate staff to man any buffets or action stations. For example, an carving station would require one person to slice the baron of beef in addition to a server to clear the room for a party of 100 guests.

Use this list to guide you as you create your event. Follow these rules of etiquette to keep your guests happy, your party running smoothly, preventing any *faux pas* from occurring.

TIPS ensure prompt service.

It is very important to scenario your guests before a meal begins as this will allow for special requests. The silent vegetarian, as we call it in banquet parlance, is never offered, but instead implied. Always have a few vegetarian plates available. If a guest at the table is vegetarian or has food allergies they will make their presence known. Also, keep in mind, if you are offering a choice of entrees you need a card for the guests to rest above their place setting to identify which option they have chosen. Never assume they will remember as they have sent their RSVP months in advance. Make sure the wait staff filters any special requests through the banquet captain so that he can relay this information to the chef, allowing the kitchen ample time to prepare them so the wait staff can serve each of the guests at a given table all at the same time.

* To scenario the guests means to introduce yourself, partner and give them a description of the menu.

ELEMENTS OF A ROOM SETUP

Details are important to the setup of your room. They are what makes your party special. I have composed a list of details that should be followed when a banquet room is being set up for a function.

1. Leave enough space at the entrance to your room so that guests can enter comfortably.
2. Tables should be staggered so that guests can easily walk through them.
3. Allow enough space around the perimeter of the room as well.
4. Be sure all chairs are set properly around your table with the head chair facing a podium, stage, buffet or other focal point in the room. If the room does not have a focal point the head chair should face the entrance to the room.

5. Be sure that tables are placed far enough away from buffets or a dance floor to give guests enough room to navigate these spaces.
6. Be sure to inspect all linen as you place it on the tabletop. Look for any holes or stains that might be on the tablecloths as this detracts from the look of the table.

7. The tablecloth should be thrown so that the crease of the cloth extends from the head chair to the chair directly across from it.
8. The cloth must hang freely, not rest on chairs.
9. All silverware should be checked for spots and polished before placement. Proper placement of the silverware is important and all silverware must form a box at each place setting with the silverware at that place setting pointing to the silverware at the place sitting directly across from it. Your silverware selection will vary depending on the courses served. Remember when the guests eat their meals they will start with the outside silverware first and work inward saving the silverware at the top of the place setting for last.

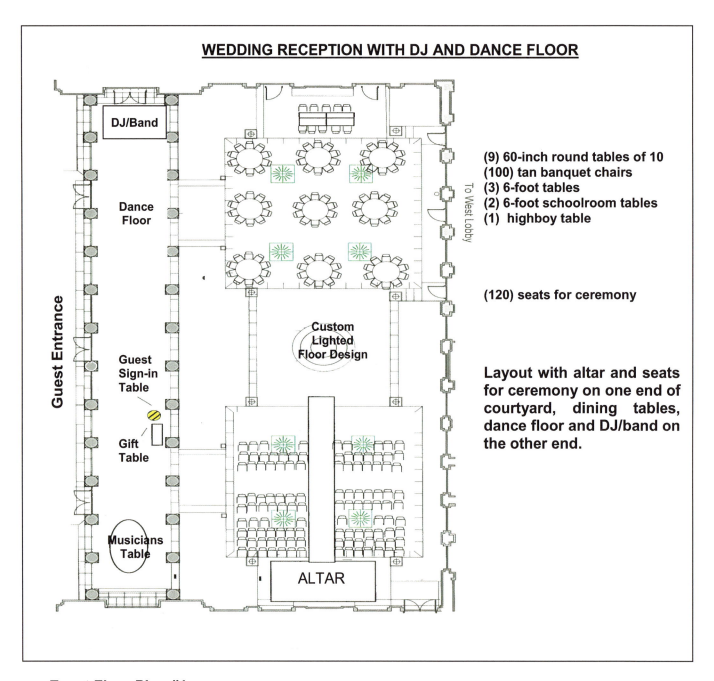

EVENTS YOU DESIGN

WEDDING RECEPTION WITH DJ AND DANCE FLOOR

DJ/Band

Dance Floor

Guest Entrance

Guest Sign-in Table

Gift Table

Musicians Table

Custom Lighted Floor Design

ALTAR

To West Lobby

(9) 60-inch round tables of 10
(100) tan banquet chairs
(3) 6-foot tables
(2) 6-foot schoolroom tables
(1) highboy table

(120) seats for ceremony

Layout with altar and seats for ceremony on one end of courtyard, dining tables, dance floor and DJ/band on the other end.

Event Floor Plan #1

12. Creamers, lemons and butters as well as goose necks of dressing should all be placed in the same location on each table. You want to place the butter knife along the edge of the butter plate so that it rests vertically on the plate. The spoon for the dressing should also rest on the edge of the salad plate that sits beneath the goose neck of dressing.

10. When china is placed on the table there should be no shadowing. China never rests atop your silverware.
11. Salt and pepper shakers and sugar caddies should be full, clean and placed directly in front of the head chair and the chair directly across at arms length on every table.

These details are important and reflect the overall look of your event. You will be able to look at the room setup and determine if it is set correctly. To put things in proper prospective, when you stand at the end of a row of set tables, every table, chair, tablecloth, number stand, centerpiece, napkin and all other items on the tabletop should line up precisely. When you set up your table at home you should follow the same guide lines.

EVENTS YOU DESIGN

Yes, you can create the ultimate party! All it takes is planning, organization and imagination. Purchase a notebook, complete the set of questions in the beginning of this section, placing all answers in your notebook. Now you have constructed a basic outline for your shindig. From this sketch you can begin to style your event. Place pictures, sample colors, keep track of representative menus, drinks, things you can do in advance, floor plans, equipment needs, all information that pertains to your event should be listed in this book. Remember that budgeting will help you to see what elements you can afford or where you need to scale down. So be sure to write your budget on paper as well.

Be sure that those who work with you are well informed by giving them a copy of all information important to the planning and setup of your event. When selecting vendors, a caterer or event planner be sure to ask them questions specific to your needs. You want to make the best possible choices. Inform your event planner of any ideas for your event so that they may create a party that you envision. If your event is on a large scale you might have a production meeting like the professionals do so that you can go over every detail with those involved in the production of your event. The point is, you want everyone to be well informed. Once you have completed these steps then you are ready to move on to the second section of this book.

In the second half of the book I have listed hundreds of ideas for decorating. I start with a brief decorating introduction and then move on to the many ideas for decorating. The ideas in this section are categorized so that you can easily locate them. Each category has a brief introduction followed by ideas which are numbered to help make it easy for you to find each one. Use these ideas to help you create a sparkling celebration.

I don't look busy because I did it right the first time

2: **DECORATING**
The beauty is in the details.

Your party reflects your taste, standards as well as your personal style. To create interest you want designs with dimension using vibrant layering and texturing of colors. Choose a palette or primary color to work with. Make your event unique with embellishments of unusual items incorporated into your flower designs. Create a stunning entrance to your party using flowers. Be as creative, innovative and fresh as possible. Custom lighting from the moon, tiki torches, little white lights and lanterns all aglow, create an ethereal intriguing mood, along with fresh foods expertly prepared and beautifully presented, synchronized service, a wedding cake with sayings on it, and a custom aisle runner with personal motifs or monograms. Other items to include might be a love birds ice sculpture, a sign with sweethearts written on it and Blanc de Blanc sparkling white wine made solely from the chardonnay grape. These ideas all come together to create the perfect affair, a picture of the perfect environment.

So where do you begin the decorating process? You need to determine your theme as this will dictate the look of your décor and your choices concerning colors, flowers, props, lighting and so on. Once you have made this decision you can start choosing a color scheme. Choosing color is a personal matter. Use a color wheel just as designers do to help you determine what colors work well together. Choose a favorite color and match it with a complimentary color.

Complimentary colors sit across from each other on the color wheel. Blue and yellow or red and green are examples of complimentary colors. Pair your favorite color with an analogous color. Analogous colors sit next to each other on the color wheel. Examples of this are: blue and purple or red and orange. Complimentary colors tend to be more formal and analogous colors are less formal. Colors set the mood, red, yellow and orange are warm colors, while green, blue and purple are cool colors. Warm colors make you feel warm. They arouse conversation and stimulate energetic actions. Cool colors tend to have a calming effect. Light colors tend to make a space look bigger while dark colors tend to make it look smaller. Select a color to work with your style, such as blue, and let your color choices follow through by utilizing different hues of that color. Take your cue from the season, utilize pastel colors for a spring event. Various elements in a room such as flowers, linen and lighting start with an exciting color. Color sets the tone of your affair so be sure that the colors you choose match the color scheme at your venue in order to create a cohesive look. Making the correct color choices will give your party a polished look.

When planning your event, have a test meal, with samples swatches of fabric in various colors available for you to view while you determine the color scheme that you want for your party. Set up an inspiration board like the designers do displaying your choices in colors with sample pictures of flowers, china, linen, glassware, silverware and napkins.

TIPS TO GUIDE YOU AS YOU DECORATE YOUR VENUE

1. Use the color wheel just as decorators do when choosing colors for your event.
2. To help you with the decorating process create an inspiration board. Pin examples of ideas that have been collected from magazines or copied from the internet onto your board, like flowers, food, lighting and color pallet. This will allow you to see how well your ideas work together.
3. Have a test meal complete with mock table setup and inspiration board to highlight the different elements of your party.
4. Fashion your event by choosing a theme for the event tying all of your elements together as you design around it and create a cohesive look. Be sure to think outside of the box. For a wedding reception, for example, dinner could be a chic soiree while the after party might have a disco theme. Create a fun and funky theme such as "Barbie" for grown ups or "Alice in Wonderland," transforming your space into a totally different environment. Create a wine tasting around Spanish wines by choosing elements such as a bar decorated with tiles, a map showcasing the wine regions of Spain, china and glassware that reflect Spain and serve small bite-sized appetizers called tapas.
5. Determine what you will decorate at your party. Dining tables, buffets, entrances and the stage are some of the things that you will want to decorate.
6. Always consider your tabletop as it is very important to tie every element together. When choosing a centerpiece it should reflect the size of the room and tables. Large spaces or tall ceilings require centerpieces to be big while small spaces require scaled down centerpieces. For a large space create centerpieces that are small on the bottom and large on the top by using a tall pillar stand. Table arrangements should not obstruct your guests' views of each other or of a head table or stage. Never mix plastic ware and china. Remember you are creating an environment so look at the whole picture

when making choices. You want to tie every aspect of your party together including the table.

7. For a wedding reception all linen and other decorations should be approved by the bride. Always use white unless otherwise specified. Keep in mind that traditional weddings start with whites and cream colors. Do not try to decorate a buffet with flowers that do not match the flowers chosen by the bride. Greenery such as leather leaf or bakers ferns are acceptable when decorating a wedding and do not interfere with the bride's color scheme or choice of flowers.

8. Repeat a pattern as a unique way to decorate your space. For example; utilize square tables, square charger plates, square plates, square flower arrangements and square candles and even use linen on your tables that has a square design imprinted on it. Use dots, stripes, flowers or any other pattern that you might like to repeat throughout your party space.

9. Do some research. Browse through magazines or the internet for additional ideas. When you choose your theme be sure elements such as linen, props, food and music are accurate.

THEMED PARTIES			
1. 70's Disco Party	(Sushi/Dim Sum)	28. Rock and Roll	(Phantom of the Opera)
2. Tapas Party (Tapas are bite-sized appetizers.)	15. Costume Party	29. At The Hop	43.Egyptian (Belly Dancer)
	16. Super Bowl Party	30. Masquerade	44. Toga Party
3. Sixties Laugh In	17. Casino Party	31. Karaoke	45. Dinner Theater
4. Winter Fest	18. Country Music	32. Winter Wonderland	46. Medieval
5. Tea Party	19. Baby Shower	33. Gone to the Dogs	47. St. Patrick's Day
6. Bar/Bat Mitzvahs	20. Mexican	34. Futuristic	48. Easter
7. Movie Theme	21. Luau	35. Wine Tasting (Spain, France, Italy)	49. Thanksgiving day
8. Broadway	22. Cabaret		50. Under the Sea
9. Country	23. Halloween	36. Gala	51. Pool Party
10. Mardi Gras Parties	24.Christmas (Collect gifts for needy children.)	37. Auction/Fundraiser	52. Progressive Dinner
11. Carnivals		38. Art or Museum	53. Cabaret
12. Martini Party		39. Automotive Theme	54. Zoo
13. Cocktail Party	25. Moroccan	40. 50's Diner	55. Harlem Renaissance
14. Asian Party	26. Celebrity Party	41. Symphony Theme	56. Italian Theme
	27. Sports Themes	42. Opera	57. Shakespeare

Remember to use your imagination when choreographing your event. Color, scheme, lighting, flowers, decorations, food, drink, music and location all team together to create a specific mood. Details are what make it unique and special. The smallest details make the biggest impression and simplicity can equate to stunning. Transform a blah space into an ah! space by choosing a contemporary design or bring opulence into your space. Tie all of the elements of your theme together to create a cohesive environment. Stage your event by adding your own personal touches to reveal your personality.

The next chapters are filled with decorating ideas for feasting tables, buffets, action stations, food displays, lighting, furniture, aisles, backdrops and more to add drama to your event. There are ideas for budgets large or small so caterers, florists, and pastry chefs alike should have no trouble utilizing these ideas in the designing of your event to create your persona. Be sure to copy any ideas that you like and take them with you when you talk with those that will be involved in making your next bash successful.

3: FOOD

I eat therefore I am.

When we gather with family and friends to celebrate a significant occurrence in life, such as a birth in the family or a wedding, food and drink naturally follow. A get together among friends sharing a repast and lively conversation requires a well thought out meal and some bottles of wine. Remember not only do we celebrate the wondrous occasions in life, but we celebrate the foods that we eat. Celebrate each individual course, enjoying the first down to the last. Keep in mind that we see our meal first, next we smell the aromas of the food and lastly we taste, so make sure that your food is served attractively and is well balanced in colors, textures and flavors.

This section of the book will help you determine what the food for your party will be and how it will be served. So what type of food do you want to share with your guests and what type of meal will you serve, brunch, reception, sit-down or buffet dinner? The time of day, style of the event such as casual, formal or themed are important to your decision. Lighter foods are great for midday functions, but an evening event requires heavier foods. If your event is planned for midday between 12 noon and two PM consider serving sandwiches and salads. If your event will be hosted between five PM and nine PM you need to serve heavier foods as in a plated or buffet dinner. You might opt to serve appetizers but make sure you have enough offerings to satisfy hungry guests. Make no mistake you will run out of food as your guests will fill their plates with food as this is supper. If you are planning a wedding reception and want to serve cake and punch only be sure to schedule the reception between two and four PM and inform guests of the food arrangements. For a dinner, it is appropriate to have a one-hour cocktail party before the dinner event takes place, serving finger foods.

There are several factors that should influence your decision:
1. Budget is a key factor. Remember to stick with the assigned and do not let others involved in your choices override it. When you speak with caterers make sure they understand this. Under no circumstances should they go over budget without your approval.
2. The size and type of event are important to your food choices. If you are over budget you should consider tweaking the guest list.
3. Keep the season in mind when creating your menu. Foods that are in season will be less expensive than those that are out of season. Also consider locally grown foods they will be less expensive and are a positive contribution to your community.

4. Remember that the number of courses served will raise your food costs and options such as dual entree will raise the cost per plate.

MEAL OPTIONS

The objective is to serve foods that taste good and are visually stunning. Seasonal foods that are fresh and celebrate the time of year in which they are abundant, expertly prepared and pleasing to the eye, are the bill of fare. You want to create the unexpected with vegetables that have texture, color, seasonality and originality. Serve foods on white plates to better showcase the food. Use parsley to liven the flavor and add green color to the plate. Remember it is all about the food. Following are some sample menu ideas and a list of ideas for beautifully displaying foods at your next affair.

BRUNCH:
If your event is scheduled to kick off in the morning, you might have a brunch. A brunch consists of breakfast foods such as omelets, breakfast meats, fresh fruit and assorted breads. Serve fresh juices or maybe a bellini which consists of peach nectar and champagne. Set up an omelet station so that guests can watch as their favorite omelet is being prepared. Be sure to have an assortment of jams and jellies and if you can find it serve plugra butter which has a lower moisture content, 80 percent butter fat and has a richer flavor. It was originally produced in Europe and can be found in the United States. If you like serve a continental breakfast which consists of various breads and pastries along with fresh squeezed juices and don't forget the coffee freshly ground and piping hot.

MIDDAY OR LUNCH:
If you are planning a midday event you may want to offer finger sandwiches, chips and dips, crudités a variety of salads and sliced fruit. Perhaps a cold crab salad, chicken salad or salad nicoise to tempt your guests and entertain their palates is in order. Be sure to include a libation from the bar such as a crisp buttery glass of chardonnay or a specialty drink created just for your event. A midday event may include a wedding, baby shower, birthday, graduation or any number of occasions to get together and celebrate life's wonderful surprises.

LATE AFTERNOON:
For a late afternoon event such as a wedding reception serve light hors d'oeuvres and wedding cake along with punch and coffee. An afternoon wedding reception is the perfect time to offer your guests a selection of hors d'oeuvres such as prosciutto wrapped melon, miniature crab cakes with remoulade sauce, crudités and dip as well as an assortment of exotic cheeses. You may want to offer a selection of tea sandwiches as a light alternative. Be creative with your choices.

EVENING:
Host a reception, buffet or sit-down dinner that consists of heavier foods. Be sure to inform your guests of the food arrangements so that they know what to expect when they arrive at your party. Never have an evening event that is light on food without informing your guests so that they do not arrive expecting a full course meal. The following information has some basics for planning a reception or sit-down dinner. Look under buffets in Chapter Two to find out more about them.

RECEPTIONS:

A reception might consist of a variety of hors d'oeuvres such as bruschetta, mushroom and goat cheese tartlets, smoked salmon on a toast point and chicken satay. Serve hors d'oeuvres in lieu of a sit-down dinner as a way to satisfy your guests' needs for nourishment. A baron of beef, a chef performance station of pasta, an Asian stir fry station as well as a variety of appetizers cold and hot to tempt the palate make for great reception food. If you have a reception in which you butler pass hors d'oeuvres you will need to serve food items that require the use of a cocktail napkin instead of a cocktail plate. Utilize small plastic serving containers or amuse bouché spoons to serve bite-sized samples of food.

Choose desserts such as miniature tarts or petits fours to display or butler pass at your reception. If you are having a wedding reception then you will probably serve wedding cake. Consider a cupcake tree or a variety of desserts such as a napoleon, crème brulee, fruit tarts and an assortment of wedding cookies as an option to the traditional wedding cake and allow guests to approach a dessert station for self service. Dessert is optional at a reception but your guests will expect sweets to complement the savory foods served to them. Friandises such as tiny cookies or petits fours will suffice if you wish to serve something sweet to your guests.

PLATED DINNERS:

Plated dinners are a more formal way to serve guests than a buffet dinner. A platted dinner would be served from five PM to nine PM. It could consist of three courses up to six courses.

You might serve a salad, entree and dessert course or you might serve an appetizer and an intermezzo, such as sorbet, to cleanse the palate along with the other courses. Soup is also an option. A plated dinner might be followed by a program or dancing. A wedding might involve light hors d'oeuvres and cocktails followed by a plated dinner, wedding cake and dancing and other wedding party antics such as garter toss and tossing of the bridal bouquet.

If you choose to have a plated dinner you will need staff to serve the dinner. A plated dinner requires more staff than a buffet dinner, but if your dinner is being held at a hotel or other banquet facility they should have an adequate number of servers to take care of your guests' needs. A hotel or banquet facility usually deems two servers per every 40 to 50 guests for a sit-down dinner and one server for every 100 guests at a reception as an adequate amount of staff to maintain superior service. Be sure that the wait staff scenarios your guests, giving them their name, placing the napkin in the guests' laps and reciting the menu to the guests. It is always important to inform the guests of what is being served for dinner. By verbally communicating the menu to the guest you allow the guest to inform the wait staff of any dietary issues they may have. Remember a guest may be a vegetarian or have specific food allergies to gluten, dairy or nuts that need to be addressed by the kitchen.

A few other options for dinner service include: dinner family style, where platters of each food item are placed directly onto the table and guests can plate their own meal and French style table service in which food is platted table side. Formal French table style service would be seen in a fine dining establishment, but would not be a feasible way to serve a large gathering of people. You might also consider serving light hors d'oeuvres and cocktails before a plated dinner.

PRICING AND BANQUET EVENT ORDER

ITEM	COST PER PERSON X TOTAL PERSONS	TOTAL COST
Food		
Cake		
Grooms Cake		
Beverages		
Misc.		
Sub Total		
Total Cost		

Chart 7

Your food cost can be calculated as: The number of guests x the cost per person. Sometimes the caterer will add an additional 10 percent over this amount to cover any extra guests that might attend unannounced. They may also add a 15 to 20 percent gratuity. Be sure to discuss these issues with your caterer to ensure you understand all of the charges on your bill.

TIP: When you receive a copy of the BEO (Banquet Event Order) make sure every detail is listed as you will only receive what has been put in writing.

TIP: Hotels and other venues offer package deals so be sure to check with them about this. Some hotels will give you a deal on food if you book a certain number of guest rooms. You might receive better pricing on food if your menu reflects the food being served at another event on the same date as yours. If you book off season or on Sunday you may receive special pricing as well. Ask the right questions!

MENU IDEAS

The ideas for menu items below will help you when determining your menu and how your food will be presented. This is just a sampling of ideas for your feast. There are certainly an infinite amount of menu items to choose from so be sure to search cookbooks and the internet to find a myriad of ideas for your big event. Look in the section on decorating under buffets for ideas for themed buffets or action stations.

Enjoy reading the sumptuous ideas and copy any that you feel would work with your event style.

Be sure to show these ideas to your caterer so that they will know what type of food presentation you would like for your event.

SALAD COURSE

Antipasto Platter

Spinach Salad with
Maple Vinaigrette

Tossed Salad with
Blue Cheese Dressing

Mixed Field Greens with
Raspberry Vinaigrette

Caesar Salad with
Peppercorn Caesar Dressing

Buffalo Mozzarella and
Beefsteak Tomatoes
with Olive Oil and Basil Drizzle

SIDE ITEMS

Potatoes Dauphine
Au Gratin Potatoes
Pommes Anna
Haricot Vert (French green beans)

Ratatouille
Braised Radicchio
Risotto
Couscous

Gnocchi
Creamy Cheese Polenta
Steamed Vegetables
Wild Rice
Five Cheeses Macaroni

SUGGESTED ENTRÉE COURSES

Chicken Kiev
Chicken Marengo
Chicken Roulade
Chicken Cordon Bleu

Beef Stroganoff
Beef Wellington
Bouquetiere of Beef
Tournedos of Beef

Salmon en Papillotte
Veal Oscar
Veal Parmigiana

Top left: Grouper, Israeli couscous with dried fruit and lemon brown-buttered cauliflower

Top right: Herb-roasted chicken with butternut *confit* and cannellini bean *cassoult*

Bottom left: Salmon with lemon caper butter and green beans

Bottom right: Salad of baby field greens, pecans, roasted peppers, tomatoes served with *lavash* cracker

CRUDITES
(Raw Vegetables)

Cherry Tomatoes
Celery
Carrots
Red and Green
Bell Peppers
Cucumbers
Asparagus
Scallions

Serve with a Ranch
or Dill dip.

ANTIPASTO PLATTER

Italian marinated artichokes, pepadew peppers, Genoa sausage, assorted roasted peppers, fresh buffalo mozzarella and Greek olive mix.

COLD CUTS

Pâtés
Salami
Parma Ham
Prosciutto

RELISH TRAY
Cornichons (gherkins)
Assorted Greek Olives
Pepperoncini
Marinated Mushrooms
Antipasti with meats:
capicola, coppa, pancetta
mortedella
and cheeses:
mozzarella, provolone
parmigiano reggiano

FRUIT TRAYS

Cantaloupe
Watermelon
Honeydew
Berries
Grapes
Pineapple
Strawberries
Apples
Kiwi

Serve with a Raspberry Yogurt dressing,
Poppy Seed dressing or Wine Cream.

Apple Almond Crème Tart

Tartlets with pastry cream, raspberries, blueberries, blackberries and mandarin orange supremes.

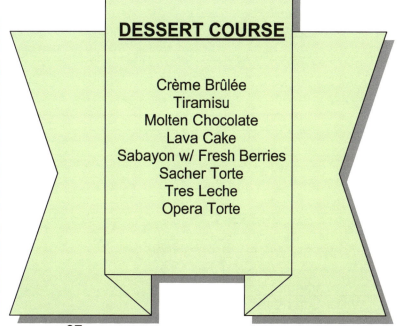

DESSERT COURSE

Crème Brûlée
Tiramisu
Molten Chocolate
Lava Cake
Sabayon w/ Fresh Berries
Sacher Torte
Tres Leche
Opera Torte

Sample Menu #1

APPETIZERS
Garlic Shrimp with Creamy Polenta
Chili and Herbs
SALAD
Arugula, Radicchio and Mache Lettuces
Fire Roasted Red and Yellow Peppers
Vine Ripened Tomato, Goat Cheese
Toasted Walnuts and Fig Vinaigrette
with Herbed Lahvosh Cracker
ENTRÉE
Grilled Filet of Beef
with Boursin Stuffed Portabella Mushroom
and Creamy Mashed Potatoes with Spinach Glaze
and Fried Leek Garnish
DESSERT
Mousse au Chocolat
DINNER WINE SELECTIONS:
Red Delas Saint Espirit Cotes du Rhone 2007
White Healdsburg
Ranches Unoaked Chardonnay 2007

Sample Menu #2

SALAD
Romaine Topped with Fresh Grated Parmigiano
Reggiano, Pine Nuts, Sun Dried Tomatoes
Garlic Croutons and
Creamy Peppercorn Caesar Dressing
ENTRÉE
Duo Entrée Bone-in Filet of Beef, Seared Scallops
with Beurre Blanc Sauce and Haricot Verts, Roasted
Fingerling Potatoes and Assorted Rolls
DESSERT
Berries in Sabayon Sauce
DINNER WINE SELECTIONS:
Red Franciscan Napa Valley
Cabernet Sauvignon 2005
White Edna Valley Chardonnay 2007

Menu #3

APPETIZER
Papaya, Mango, Mint, Basil, Cilantro
Garlic Wrapped in Rice Paper and
Deep Fried with an Asian Dipping Sauce
Shrimp Wrapped in Wontons Deep Fried
with a Peanut Butter Dipping Sauce
ENTRÉE
Asian Seared Beef Tenderloin
Spicy Grilled Eggplant and Fried Rice
DESSERT
Asian Pear Sorbet with a Coconut Almond Cookie
DINNER WINES:
Murai Daiginjo Sake
Red Rusden Barossa Valley
Boundaries Sauvignon 2004
White Nautilus Sauvignon Blanc
Marlborough 2008

Menu #4

Reception Butler Passed

APPETIZERS
Cucumber Hearts with Chevre (goat cheese)
and Sun Dried Tomatoes
Crudités with Dill Dip
Skewered Grilled Eggplant and Summer Squash
Peppadew Peppers Stuffed with Chevre and Topped
with Pine Nuts
ENTRÉE
Skewered Grilled Shrimp
Beef Sate with Teriyaki Sauce
Pancetta Wrapped Pork Roast
Heart Shaped Crostini with Tomatoes and Basil
Place bunches of herbs on trays for garnish.

DESSERTS
Chocolate Heart Shaped Butter Cookies
Long Stemmed Strawberries Passed with the Cake
BEVERAGES
Champagne
Non-Alcoholic Choices of Sodas and Bottled Water

Menu #5
Reception Buffet

APPETIZERS
Crudités with Dip
Assorted Dips such as: Olive Tapenade, Crab Dip
Artichoke Dip with Chips, Pita and Toast Points
Roasted Vegetables with Parmesan
and Balsamic Drizzle
Baked Brie
Frico Tacos
Shrimp on Ice
Tomato Basil Olive Tartlet
Prosciutto Wrapped Bread Sticks
Baron of Beef
DESSERTS
Sugar Cookies Glazed on the Diagonal
with Pale Pink Icing*
Chocolate and White Wedding Cake
Amuse Bouché Spoons with Assorted Mousses or
Cheese Cake Mousse.
DRINKS
Slush Punch
Kendall Jackson Chardonnay
Shiraz or Merlot
Berenger White Zinfandel , Beer, Coffee

*Have your baker design cookies or a cake to match
your events theme.

Menu #6

Reception Buffet

APPETIZERS
Crudités
Fruit and Baked Brie
Artichoke Dip
Shrimp
Beef Tenderloin
Chicken Satay
Tomato and Red Pepper Pasata
Bruschetta
Crudités
Fruit and Baked Brie
Artichoke Dip
Shrimp
Beef Tenderloin
DESSERTS
Bride's Cake, Groom's Cake
BEVERAGES
Bottled Water, Sodas, Punch
Coffee, Beer, Wine and Champagne

(*Mise en place* in French is the
order of things as it pertains to food.)

CHEESES: Caveman Blue-bottom left hand corner. Top left hand corner is Triple Cream Brie alongside Smoked Gouda complimented with grapes. Raclette, from Switzerland, is in the upper right hand corner above the apricots. Boursin is the three scoops of cheese and next Marcona Almonds.

CHEESE DISPLAYS AND DESSERT CHEESE DISPLAYS

This page has some basic information on choosing cheeses and Chart 8 which showcases a sampling of cheeses along with wine pairings. When you go to a banquet function often times the same cheeses are served. Have the chef choose cheeses that are out of the norm. If you are preparing a cheese display for your event ask the cheese monger at your local cheese shop to help you make choices. Cheese can be costly. Be sure to visit a reputable cheese monger when purchasing cheeses; you want to ensure that the cheeses you are purchasing are fresh and have not sat in the store for long periods of time. Also important is the ability of the cheese monger to slice cheeses straight from the block of cheese. Many shops offer cheeses already precut and wrapped. Stick with the former if you can.

Cheeses are a wonderful addition to your meal. If you are serving a heavy meal allow one ounce to one and one-half ounces of cheese per guest. If the meal being served is on the light side allow two ounces to three ounces per guest. This allows enough cheese for each guest to have a nice sampling. Some other things to keep in mind are:

1. Serve chesses at 70 degrees (room temperature).
2. Place cheeses on your platter in order of mildest to strongest. Let your guests choose which they prefer to start with.
3. Utilize an odd number of cheeses. The "Rule of Three" seems to be a popular trend and the principals of Feng Shui support this idea.
4. Serve slices or cubes of cheese. For a wedge of cheese supply a knife in which to cut the cheese. For a Brie or Boursin also have a knife available.
5. For a dessert cheese display serve wine or ports which are dessert wines fortified with brandy.
6. Be sure to place the tag or sign next to each cheese identifying each one. Remember to have accompaniments to go along with your cheeses. Place crackers, French bread, baguettes, butter, quince paste alongside of your cheeses. Grapes, figs, apples, pears, fresh berries and nuts also go well with cheese. Chart 8 gives examples for cheese displays, remember you can serve any cheese with dessert. In Europe dessert cheeses are served after dinner so consider this option.

Keep this information on hand when deciding how to put together a wine tasting. You might also add chocolates to a wine tasting along with all of the other goodies. Chart 8 gives a sampling of cheeses that you might choose for your next event and also lists some wine pairings.

Cheese	Country	Milk/ Type	Taste/Texture	Wine
Mozzarella	Originally produced in Italy	Cow's Milk	Soft Texture Mild Flavor	Sauvignon Blanc, Semillon
Brie	France	Cow's Milk	Soft-ripened	Chardonnay, Pinot Gris, Riesling
Triple Cream Brie	France	Cow's Milk	Soft-ripened	Chardonnay, Pinot Gris, Riesling
Boursin Aux Fines Herbs	France	Cow's Milk' Cream	Garlic, Salt, Pepper, Parsley and Chives	Beaujoalis
Manchego	Spain	Sheep's Milk	Mild, Salty, Nutty Flavor	Cabernet, Bordeaux
Colby	USA	Cow's Milk	Semi-hard, Soft, Moist and Mild	Cabernet, Bordeaux
Fontina	Italy	Cow's Milk	Semi-soft, Pungent, Intense Flavor	Cabernet, Bordeaux, Chianti
Raclette	Switzerland	Cow's Milk	Semi-firm	Gewurztraminer, Riesling
Reypenaer VSOP (Gouda)	Netherlands	Cow's Milk	Hard Texture, Sharp and Tangy	Cabernet, Bordeaux
Parmigiano	Italy	Cow's Milk	Hard Texture	Cabernet, Sauvignon, Bordeaux
Pecorino Romano	Italy	Sheep's Milk	Hard, Strong Sheep Flavor	Cabernet, Sauvignon, Bordeaux
Gorgonzola	Italy	Cow's Milk	Rich, Creamy, Pungent Flavor	Cabernet, Sauvignon, Bordeaux
Humboldt Fog (Goat Cheese)	USA	Goat's Milk	Gooey with a Cream Cheese Center, Butter and Cream Flavors	Zinfandel, Pinot Noir
Coulommiers	France	Cow's Milk	Buttery Color and Supple Texture with a Nutty Flavor	Red Wine from Bordeaux, Cotes du Rhone or Languedoc
Camambert	France	Cow's Milk	Delicate, Salty Taste and a Clear Yellow Paste	Red Bordeaux or Beaujolais
Farmhouse Cheddar	England	Cow's Milk	Fruity, Flowery, Nutty and Sugary	Claret, a Red Wine from the Bordeaux Region of France
Blue Stilton	Britain	Cow's Milk	Crumbles Easily with a Strong Odor	Port Wine

Chart 8

FOOD
110 Ideas for Attractive Food Displays

> **A basic dressing equals one part balsamic vinegar and three parts olive oil.**

The following ideas are designed to give you plenty of ideas for attractively displaying your food. Adapt these ideas to fit your needs. Talk to a caterer so that they can help you determine which will work best with your theme and budget.

> **Roux: Equal parts butter to flour. Use 1 tablespoon of butter to 1 tablespoon of flour. The roux is used to thicken sauces, soups and gumbo.**

1. **TIP: Choose organic foods that are locally grown. What raises the cost of organics is the certification that comes along with labeling your products organic. Many farmers grow organic produce, but cannot afford the label. Do some research to see if you can locate farmers who grow foods organically even though their products are not labeled organic.**
2. Create a beautiful bread display for your table by placing loaves of artisan breads in a decorative basket and setting them in the center of your table or buffet.
3. Make a loaf of bread with a specific design such as initials or a flower to place as a centerpiece on your buffet.
4. Utilize decorative baskets to display crackers, sliced breads or bread sticks.
5. For a wonderful table display, bake a wreath out of bread dough and display it in the table's center.
6. For a small breadbasket be sure to line the inside with an envelope folded napkin. Set rolls and slices of bread inside of the napkin fold or arrange bread sticks so that they peek through the napkin fold.
7. For a unique way of serving bread sticks place them standing upright in a cylindrical glass vase and set them in the middle of each dining table.
8. For a chic look at your dinner party fill bowls with bread sticks and crostini and place them on your dinner table.
9. Use decorative baskets to hold your crudités display. Create bowls of various dips to go with your vegetables.
10. Create a pineapple tree to display your skewered foods or satay. To create the tree merely cut the bottom of the pineapple off so that the pineapple sits flat on your food platter. Use decorative picks to skewer food items and secure them into the pineapple tree.
11. Use a cantaloupe or honeydew to beautifully display skewered appetizers. Cut the bottom of the melon off so that the fruit sits flat on your platter. Line with leaf lettuce and sit the melon flat side down in the center of the lettuce. Insert the skewered appetizers into the melon at various intervals.
12. Create a melon bowl by cutting the top and bottom of your cantaloupe or honey dew off. One end of the melon will be the bottom of your bowl. When you cut this end off cut just enough so that the bowl will set level. You do not want to cut too much off of the melon in order to create the hole. You will be

filling the bowl with a dip for your fruit. Once the top has been removed you want to scoop out the melon with a melon baller. Use frill picks to skewer the melon balls and insert them into the sides of the melon. Set the melon on a platter as above and arrange appetizers around the base of the melon. Fill the melon with a sauce to dip the appetizers in. Arrange fruit around the base of the melon and fill the melon with a dipping sauce such as a wine cream.

> **To create a balsamic drizzle, over a low heat, reduce four bottles of balsamic vinegar down to one bottle. The finished product will be thick like syrup.**

13. Use a watermelon to create a fruit bowl. You can create many designs such as a boat, a whale, fish, a swan, a bowl with a handle or a baby carriage just to name a few. Hollow out the watermelon by carving the desired design out of the rind. Purchase a book that gives instructions on how to do this or create a template to guide you as you cut your design out of the rind. Use a melon ball scoop to remove the flesh from your melon and reserve the melon balls as part of your fruit salad. Fill the hollowed out melon with fruit salad and place in the center of your table display. Also reserve some of the melon balls or other cut fruits and adhere them to the outside of your melon with frill picks as a creative way to decorate your bowl.

14. A bread bowl is a decorative way to serve dips such as spinach and artichoke or a ranch dip. Create your bowl with a round loaf of sour dough bread by cutting off the top with a serrated knife. Cut a circle around the inside edge of the bread and pull the center of the loaf out, leaving a hollow opening. Center your bread bowl on a large platter and arrange tortilla chips or vegetables around the bowl. Fill the bowl with your dip.

15. To set up a fondue station skewer vegetables and meats ahead of time. Utilize a deep fryer as a way for your guests to cook the food items. Place cheese fondue into a crock pot for self service.

16. For your crudités display hollow out a red cabbage and use the cabbage as a bowl for your dip. In France crudités means an appetizer consisting of shredded vegetables dressed in a vinaigrette. In America crudités is a marketing term for the food service industry to describe a raw vegetable tray.

17. For a unique presentation cover trays for your appetizers with leaves instead of doilies.

18. For a unique way to serve appetizers buy a picture frame and insert a picture, or a fabric with a design, into the frame. Choose a fabric or paper to match your theme. Arrange your appetizers on the glass of the frame for a platter to remember.

Use a thinner noodle for tomato sauce.
Use a thicker noodle for cream sauce.

19. Utilize amuse bouché spoons to serve bite-sized morsels of food to your guests. An amuse bouché is a bite-sized piece of food. An amuse bouché spoon is similar to a soup spoon, upon which is served a tiny morsel of food.

Amuse bouché in French means "amuses the mouth."

20. For a crudités display on a tray utilize leaf lettuce to line your platter.

21. Use a silver tray to attractively display tea sandwiches. Place a garnish of flowers created from vegetables such as tomatoes or radishes on the silver tray. Purchase a book on how to create garnishes.

Archestratus was a Greek author from the 3rd Century BC who invented recipes.

22. Leaf lettuce makes a great backdrop for canapés arranged on a tray. Place a cup made out of head lettuce in the center of your platter for olives to rest in.
23. Make a bouquet of roses from tomato skins and use greenery for leaves. Go to amazon.com or your local book store to purchase books on garnishing.
24. Pineapples are wonderful by themselves. They make great bases to secure flowers made from vegetables. Be sure to keep the top of the pineapple intact and cut off the bottom of the pineapple so that it will have a flat base to sit on. Arrange your flowers below the crown of the pineapple securing them with toothpicks. What a wow decoration for your buffet table or even for a dinner table centerpiece.
25. Use wooden cutting boards to attractively display canapés and other appetizers.
26. Use metal or wire tiered basket stands to display breads, fruits or vegetables on your buffet table.
27. Place skewered foods on trays to display or butler pass to your guests.
28. For a clever way to create tea sandwiches cut the sandwich bread into various shapes. Use a cookie cutter in a heart shape to create sandwiches for a wedding reception.
29. When decorating trays of food to butler pass use fresh parsley, dill, rosemary, mint or other fresh herbs. You could create mini bunches of herbs tied off with ribbon to use for your butler passed food items. Also use fresh flowers as a form of garnishment.
30. For a special touch, purchase unusual picks, to skewer foods for your hors d'oeuvre display.

Trinity consists of garlic, green pepper and onion, celery and pepper.

31. Use bouillon (soup) spoons to serve bite-sized hors d'oeuvres. Arrange the spoons on colorful platters and butler pass them at your reception.
32. For a platter of appetizers utilize rose petals to cover your platter before setting the food items on the platter.
33. Utilize glass pebbles to layer the bottom of your serving tray and arrange your appetizers on top of the pebbles.
34. Utilize Chinese soup spoons for bite-sized morsels of food.

Mirepoix: Parsley, thyme and bay leaf are the basic herbs utilized when making stocks.

35. For a unique way to serve cold soup such as gazpacho fill an oval tray with crushed ice and arrange small shot glasses of soup in the crushed ice.
36. You can purchase acrylic trays designed with holes in them so that paper cones fit snugly in the holes. Fill the paper cones with food items such as french fries or sweet potato chips. This is a great

way to butler pass hors d'oeuvres.

37. Utilize small wooden Popsicle spoons to serve tiny bite-sized morsels of food. Monogram the wooden spoons with the initials of the bride and groom for a wedding reception.
38. Utilize bowls to display small slices of pizza, tarts or flat breads covered with cheese.
39. Decorate a square acrylic tray with gold trim and beads for a pretty serving tray for appetizers.
40. Place a spoon full of dip into the bottom of a vodka glass and stand raw vegetables upright in the dip in a lovely arrangement.
41. Utilize a large martini glass to display and butler pass satay and other skewered foods.
42. Utilize lemon grass, chives or banana leaves as part of your appetizer display by laying them on a clear glass serving platter.
43. For before the meal enjoyment, place platters of tapas on your table. Tapas are appetizers served with alcoholic beverages. They originated in Spain.

The Italians use the word "prosciutto" to apply to all hams.

44. Utilize fig or hydrangea leaves to cover a tray for serving appetizers.
45. Utilize a hollowed out orange, lemon or lime to serve your sorbet for an intermezzo. The intermezzo is served between courses when needed to cleanse the palate.
46. For a wedding reception purchase heart shaped plates or platters to serve your food on.
47. To serve your appetizers in style utilize miniature plastic dishes in various shapes, placing the appetizers on the plates and arranging them on trays for service. For a dish that has been sitting add fresh herbs just before serving.

The beauty of a spoon is breathtaking. **Andrée Putman**

48. Place plates of appetizers in the center of each table for guests to enjoy before the meal.
49. Create tea sandwiches in which you cut a heart out of the center of the top layer of bread.
50. For a fabulous sea food display utilize a glow light to place in the center of your buffet. The glow light is actually a base that has a light nestled inside of it to light up the plastic tray that sits on top of it. You can use colored gels to change the color of the glow light. The large plastic tray that sits atop the base has a hole in the bottom of the tray in which to attach a hose to drain any excess water. Ice is placed in the tray and seafood is arranged on top of the ice to create a decorative seafood display. You can purchase a glow light from any restaurant supply store.
51. Utilize bowls carved from ice to display your seafood. Keep in mind that this would be a job for a professional as they have the experience and the equipment with which to do the carving. If you have your event at a banquet facility they should have the means to carve anything you could desire from a block of ice!
52. Use a canoe filled with ice to display seafood on a buffet.
53. Maybe you cannot carve your own ice sculpture, but you can still have one at your next party. For an easy and inexpensive ice sculpture purchase small plastic molds from a restaurant supply company.

You can find molds shaped like dolphins or fish.

54. For a unique and stunning way to serve seafood have a freestanding oyster bar carved out of ice for your oysters and other seafood. The oyster bar can be lit and initials or insignia carved into the front of the bar. Most venues can offer ice carvings and will be happy to accommodate your request.

Let thy food be thy medicine. **Hippocrates 400 BC**

55. **TIP: For a cold food display create a rectangular frame out of wood or metal strips. Set bags of ice inside of the frame. Cover the bags of ice with a cloth or leaves. Place your bowls of cold food items such as salads on top of the ice to keep them cold. This is an easy and inexpensive way to display and keep cold foods cold.**

56. For a unique salad presentation utilize a glow light filling the tray of the glow light with shaved ice and arrange glass bowls of cold salads on top of the shaved ice. Turn on the glow light for a shimmering presentation. The glow light is made of plastic. The base houses a light to illuminate the tray that sits on top of it and has a cord that plugs into an electrical outlet. The tray that sits on top is two inches deep and can be filled with ice in order to keep cold foods cold. The tray also has a spigot attached so that a hose can be screwed onto it for draining water into a bucket.

57. Have the chef create an ice sculpture with flowers inside of the ice.

Equation for salad dressings: 16 tablespoons = one cup / one cup = eight orders

58. Have the chef carve a heart with love birds sitting on the top of the heart out of ice. There are companies that will carve an ice sculpture for events with prices ranging from moderate to expensive.

> ## BASIL PESTO
>
> **Pesto consists of garlic, olive oil, basil and pine nuts. Pesto can be used on pasta, crostini breads or sandwiches. Classic pesto is created with basil leaves but you can substitute other ingredients such as cilantro.**
>
> **2 c. fresh basil leaves**
> **2 lg. cloves garlic**
> **½ c. pine nuts**
> **¼ c. freshly grated Parmesan cheese**
> **¾ tsp salt**
> **freshly ground pepper**
> **½ c. olive oil**
>
> **Place all of the ingredients into a food processor and blend until smooth. Serve in a bowl with crostini bread or spread the pesto on each slice of crostini bread and arrange on a platter.**

59. Have the chef carve an ice bowl to hold your steamed shrimp and shot glasses of gazpacho. Fill the bowl with crushed ice. Place a bowl of lemons in the center of the bowl and arrange the gazpacho around the bowl of lemons. Place the shrimp on the ice around the outer perimeter of the ice bowl.

60. Be creative when choosing containers to display your foods and beverages.

61. Have your chef create square bowls out of ice to display cut fruit for a buffet. Arrange cubed fruits such as pineapple, cantaloupe, honeydew, and oranges in bowls, placing each fruit in a different one. Place the bowls in a glow light. Fill the bowls with crushed ice to prevent melting. If possible have an audio visual person direct colored lights onto the bowls from the ceiling to create a stand out feature.

> In French cuisine there are five Mother Sauces: Cold, egg yolk and butter, white, brown and other sauces. From the Mother Sauces all other sauces evolve. Mayonnaise is a derivative of cold sauces, Hollandaise and Béarnaise are derivatives of egg yolk and butter sauces. Béchamel and Veloute are derivatives of white sauces, Bordelaise is a derivative of brown sauces and Beurre Blanc is a derivative of other sauces.

62. For a picnic that is easy to serve, line a basket with a cloth towel and fill it full of goodies to eat. Arrange meats such as bologna, sausages, wheels of cheese, bunches of grapes, olives and breads in your basket for a ready to serve picnic.

63. For a light food display for your afternoon event set up a table filled with fresh cheeses, pâtés, sausages, bolognas, olives, cornichons, fruits and breads.

64. Place accoutrements such as olives, truffles, figs, nuts and fruits in individual bowls and arrange the bowls in a shallow basket as an edible display on your buffet table.

65. Use a large shallow basket lined with a cloth towel to display pastries for your breakfast buffet.

66. Set up a table just to display fruit, cheeses, vegetables and dips.

67. Utilize a variety of containers to display crudités.

68. For a romantic fruit display for your wedding reception, carve a heart with love birds out of a watermelon rind to place on your fruit tray. This is a great centerpiece for your buffet table.

69. For your buffet table, display cut fruits in baskets of various diameters that have been stacked at different levels using glass elevations.

70. Create individual baskets or plates of crudités for each dining table.

71. For a great food display on your buffet table, utilize mirrors of various diameters, arranging food on the mirrors and stacking them largest to smallest one atop the other with rock glasses.

> BOUQUET GARNI: Carrots, celery and onions utilized to flavor stocks, soups and stews. They are placed in cheesecloth and tied off so that they may be removed after the cooking process has finished.

72. Stack platters of various diameters on top of each other by using rock glasses for the elevation. Be sure to place the largest platter on the bottom and the smallest platter on the top. Arrange your food items on the individual platters. This is a great centerpiece for your buffet table.

73. For a classic look, elevate slabs of marble of various sizes at different heights, and arrange your cold hors d'oeuvres on the marble slabs.
74. For a beautiful display for your buffet table, place tall glass cylinders filled with fruits or vegetables in the center of your buffet. Elevate platters or mirrors of various sizes around the glass cylinders. Arrange vegetables, fruits or other food items on the platters or glass mirrors.

Healthy living through food.

75. Place tall glass cylinders filled with cut fruit in the center of your buffet table. Elevate glass mirrors of various sizes on metal stands around the glass cylinders and arrange cut fruit or petits fours on the glass mirrors.
76. Utilize glass mirrors of various diameters and elevate them one atop the other starting with the largest on the bottom and the smallest on the top. Arrange shot glasses of flavored mousses on the mirrors. Use glasses as a way to elevate your mirrors.
77. To decorate the top of a tiered mirror display, place a bowl of fruits or vegetables on the top mirror of your display. Utilize whole fruits and vegetables or cut fruits and vegetables for your decoration.
78. For a lavish buffet table display arrange fruits, chesses and crackers on a unique platter and elevate in the center of your buffet table.
79. Display foods such as charcuterie or hors d'oeuvres on mirrors for a wow effect on your buffet! Charcuterie are prepared or cured meats such as prosciutto, salami or coppa and pâtés.
80. For a wine tasting set up a separate table for your food items. Serve baked Brie cheese on a tray surrounded by whole fruits such as apples, pears and grapes. Disperse wine glasses and bottles of wine throughout your display.
81. Utilize a tiered plate stand to create a focal point for your buffet. Place plates of arranged shot glasses filled with gazpacho or mousse on the plate stand.
82. Utilize the tiered plate stand to showcase plates of small bites of foods served attractively on amuse bouché spoons.
83. For an action station consisting of Chinese food have Chinese to-go boxes and chopsticks positioned on the station so that the chef can serve the guests food selections in the Chinese to-go boxes and the guest can use the chops sticks to eat with if they wish to do so.
84. Create a beautiful vegetable or fruit display by setting up a single table covered with a tablecloth and arrange your produce to resemble a farmers market. Remember to strategically place bowls of dips in your arrangement.

Pommes frites in French are french fries.

85. For a unique wine tasting set up a 6-foot table and cover it with linen. Line the table at intervals with bottles of wine and scatter fruits, cheeses and crackers down the length of the table for your guest's enjoyment. At a wine tasting always provide a spit bucket, pitchers of water and glasses, wine glasses of various shapes and sizes and a pen and note pad.
86. For a twist on a fruit and vegetable display, position a clothed tallboy table in the middle of your re-

ception area, on one side of the table create a display of vegetables and on the other side create a display of fruits complete with dips for your guests to enjoy.

87. **TIP: Generally on a banquet function where beef is being served it is cooked to a medium rare temperature, but have some available that is cooked well done for varying tastes.**

88. For a Chinese stir fry station utilize chopsticks engraved with the initials of the bride and groom and the date of the event.

89. For a Chinese style party, utilize bento boxes, chopsticks, serve miso soup, sushi and edamame. Use lanterns and Chinese hats. Offer fortune cookies to your guests with special personalized messages inside of the cookie.

RATIOS: One dozen appetizers for five people. Five dozen appetizers for 25 people.

90. For a southern tradition serve Krystal hamburgers at the end of your wedding reception so that the guests can take something to eat as they leave the party.

91. **TIP: Have boxed meals prepared for your guests to take home as they leave your wedding reception. This is a great way to send your guests off as they depart.**

92. Serve the bride and groom appetizers and drinks while riding in the limousine to the reception.

93. Purchase chopsticks in colors to match your color scheme.

94. **TIP: To help your guests find their way through a myriad of food stations print out menus and maps designating what each food station is and where it is located.**

95. For a cocktail party serve a few offerings such as crostini bread with olive tapenade or spinach and artichoke dip along with crab cakes or shrimp cocktail. Utilize salamis, cheeses, Marcona almonds and various olives to finish off your food offerings and save preparation time. Serve an assortment of cookies or petits fours as a dessert option.

To sauté: In French to jump. You need really high heat.

96. Create a party featuring different nationalities. Food, décor and music can reflect different nationalities. Set up four different areas in your event space allowing each to represent each nationality.

97. Create a display for your appetizers by elevating round Plexiglass discs of various sizes one atop the other with glasses. Place candles and vases with flowers on each tier and arrange food around them.

98. **TIP: Place signs that denote your cheese selections, flavor notes and where they come from beside your cheese tray.**

99. Be sure to use greens such as leaf lettuce to decorate a display of salads or toppings.

Utilize locally sourced foods.

100. Serve a trio of soups in shot glasses.

101. Place an artichoke folded napkin on top of a salad plate and set your soup cup on it for a nicer presentation than just a soup cup sitting on top of a saucer.

Ophelia to Hamlet, as she handed him the herb: *"There's rosemary,*
that is for remembrance; pray you, love, remember." **From Shakespeare's play,** *Hamlet*

102. For your next seafood display have the chef carve words out of ice such as JOY, LOVE or even SEAFOOD.

103. Create the wow factor at your next event, by having a caviar and lobster station. Let the chef carve stackable boxes out of ice to display your caviar, lobster or other seafood. Create an ice sculpture such as a column for the center of your display.

104. Create a sushi bar for your next event. Have the chef create blocks of ice for your sushi to rest upon and a pedestal with a logo or initials for a centerpiece.

105. For a unique food presentation use a cutting board or other large tray to create a tall mound or tower of strawberries on one end and a mound or tower of shrimp on the other. Arrange accoutrements around the towers. Set this display on your buffet or a separate station for your guests to nibble on.

106. Create a beautiful wedding fruit display utilizing a watermelon to create a sculpture of two love birds kissing. Display various fruits and even bowls of dip around the sculpture.

107. TIP: Serve your guests soup and salad before the entrée course. Have the chef place a bread bowl filled with the soup of your choice and a small salad together on the same plate.

108. Synchronized service is an elegant way to serve your guests. As each course is served the wait staff forms a line in the back hallway, one plate of food in each hand, waiting for the cue to enter the room. The staff follows a predetermined pathway through the room to their assigned table and stands at the head chair waiting for the signal to serve the food. Service continues until everyone in the room has received that course. Remember always serve food from the left side of the guest with the left hand. At a formal event be sure everyone at a table has finished eating before that course is cleared. Never cherry pick, this is not acceptable at a formal event. Cherry picking is simply removing a plate from the guest's place setting as each one finishes eating as opposed to clearing an entire table all at once. Synchronized service works best for a small event.

109. Have the chef create a special meal for your guests by serving lamb chops that have been French boned and cover the bones with frill picks that have been monogrammed with the initials of the bride and groom.

110. For a unique way of decorating your cheese display carve designs into a wheel of parmesan cheese.

TIP: For each course served at a tasting have the chef place a sample plate on top of an elevation in the center of the table. This gives each guest a chance to view that particular option for that course while critiquing it.

4: DESSERTS

"But how will I eat cake if my head is over there, and my hands are over here?"
Marie Antoinette

Dessert is a sweet ending to a fabulous meal. Spoil your guests with sweets that they will not soon forget. Dessert offerings might echo the theme of your event such as baklava served after a middle eastern meal of moussaka and a Greek salad. Follow the meal with a toast and ouzo, an anise flavored liquor from Greece. Ouzo is considered a digestif which aids the digestion after a meal has been eaten. Serve the guest of honor their favorite dessert. Serve a dessert created from a recipe that grandma often served at dinner when you were a child. Offer a variety of sweets, so that guests can choose their own favorites, by serving samples of desserts on tiny plastic cups designed for this purpose. Use your imagination for desserts that will wow your guests and leave them with a memorable impression long after your event is over.

The list following includes ideas for decorative elements, displays, various options and even a few dessert recipes that you might try at your next party. Use these ideas to create imaginative desserts that are visually stunning as well as tasteful. Be sure to share any of the ideas that you like with your caterer so he or she can help you create the perfect dessert for your party.

A List of 72 Ideas for Attractively Displaying Desserts

1. For a way to display a cake or cakes for a buffet table, fill clear glass cylindrical vases of various sizes with fruit. Rest the cakes on plates on top of the glass vases.
2. For your next Valentines Day party, bake heart shaped cookies, ice them and pipe messages on the face of the cookies such as I LOVE YOU and BE MINE. Wrap each cookie in plastic bags or cellophane and tie them off with shiny red garland hearts or ribbon.
3. Create a tiered display of cupcakes. Line the trays of various size cake stands with leaves. Stack the cake stands on top of each other placing the largest on the bottom and the smallest on the top. Arrange the cupcakes on the stands. Insert fresh flowers in between each cupcake.
4. For a birthday party have your baker design the birthday cake with the guest of honor's picture on the top of the cake. Use a favorite childhood picture if the guest of honor is an adult.
5. Use various candies to decorate a child's birthday cake.
6. Arrange cupcakes on individual paper doilies.

7. For a baby shower have a baker create a cake that has baby pictures of the mom and dad on the top of the cake. A baker can turn your print image into an edible image; also a grocery store bakery can.

8. Arrange miniature desserts on trays for display on your dessert bar.

9. Set plates or trays of miniature desserts in the middle of each dinner table for your guests to enjoy.

10. Have the pastry chef utilize small cups and plates to create the bite-sized desserts.

11. For a birthday or corporate event, have the pastry chef place the initials of the guest of honor or the company logo onto salad plates with cocoa or chocolate. Arrange the desserts onto the salad plates.

12. Have an elegant cheese display on your dessert bar.

13. For a delicious party favor cover pretzel sticks in dark and light chocolate. Roll them in various crushed candies or sprinkles.

14. As part of a dessert display for a child's party have a chocolate fountain setup and let them dip pretzels into the chocolate. Have bowls of various crushed candies or nonpareils for the children to dip the chocolate covered pretzels into.

15. You can embellish chocolate covered pretzel sticks with icing in the color of your wedding cake icing.

16. For a light and easy dessert offering serve your guests a macedoine of fresh fruit. Cut into bite-sized pieces a mixture of fruits such as pineapple, strawberries, cantaloupe and honey dew melon and place in a bowl along with fresh blueberries or raspberries in season. Mix and sprinkle with Pernod, let the fruit rest in the refrigerator to infuse the flavors. Place the fruit in coupe glasses when you are ready to serve your guests. Garnish each dessert with a fan of thin apple slices and a piece of mint leaf. Enjoy!

17. Create a magical look by adhering crystals to your glass cake stand.

18. Layer different sorbets or granitas in clear martini or Collins glasses for service.

RASPBERRY COULIS
one and one-half cups fresh raspberries , half-cup Frambois
Puree the raspberries and strain to remove the seeds. Pour into a sauce pan
and add the Frambois. Mix and simmer to reduce until thickened.

19. Have your baker create cupcakes with icing flowers on top.

20. A Baked Alaska makes a great dessert. Create individual Baked Alaskas or one large Baked Alaska to serve an entire table. Have the wait staff parade the Baked Alaskas around the room and then serve them to each individual table. Decorate the Baked Alaskas with glow sticks before parading them through the room. The chef will brown the Baked Alaskas before they go into the room.

21. A Baked Alaska, in case you are not familiar with this dessert, consists of layers of cake and ice cream covered with an outer shell of meringue. The meringue when flambéd acts as an insulator protecting the ice cream and keeping it from melting. You could put the Baked Alaska under a broiler to brown the meringue or flambé the meringue which is done by first heating your rum in a pan on the stove and igniting it and then pouring it over the Baked Alaska to brown the meringue. The rum also imparts a nice flavor to the Baked Alaska.

QUICK AND EASY BAKED ALASKA
This is an easy way to create an elegant Baked Alaska for your next party.
1 Sara Lee pound cake (in the freezer section of the grocery)
1 box of Ice Cream (flavor of your choice or use Neapolitan)
4 egg whites, at room temperature
1/3 cup sugar
1/8 teaspoon salt
Rum

Remove the pound cake from the box. Slice the cake in half horizontally while the cake is still frozen. This will make the cake easier to cut. Lay the bottom of the cake on a sheet pan or platter and arrange enough scoops of ice cream to cover the bottom half. If you are going to place the cake under a broiler make sure you place the cake on a sheet pan. After you have covered the bottom half of the cake with the scoops of ice cream place the top layer over the ice cream pressing down gently to flatten the ice cream slightly and hold the top layer in place. Put the cake in the freezer while you make the meringue topping. Put the room temperature egg whites into a mixing bowl. With a whisk or beaters whip the egg whites briefly and then add the sugar and the salt and continue to whip until stiff peaks form. Take your cake out of the freezer. Use a spatula to cover it with the meringue reserving some of the meringue to pipe a decorative boarder around the bottom and top of the cake using a star tip. Heat a small amount of the rum on the stove. Sprinkle the rum over the Baked Alaska. Place the Baked Alaska in the oven under the broiler or use a torch and brown the meringue. Put the Baked Alaska back into the freezer until you are ready to serve your dessert. Remember when you use the torch you need to be very careful as the rum will catch fire and can cause a serious accident. Always have a fire extinguisher nearby.

22. Pound cake is great for making Baked Alaska. For a twist on the recipe above, cut hearts out of the pound cake, assemble as above.

TIP: Safety is important. Make no mistake, if you do not use caution injuries could be inflicted upon yourself or a guest. Any action stations that require a burner with fuel cartridges needs to have a fire extinguisher on it. Check any burners used before placing them on a station to ensure they work properly. Remember never put your face directly above the burner when you turn it on as this could result in burns to your face.
TIP: If Sterno (fuel) for chafers is used, keep lids on hand to extinguish them. Never "blow" them out as this will cause the flames to spread possibly creating injury as well as setting fire to tablecloths and skirts. Remember Sterno canisters get hot so do not remove them from the rest beneath the chafing dish until they cool and do not place them directly on the tabletop or they will melt the fabric beneath.

23. Create dessert tiers using a metal stand that is designed to hold several platters of food. Place cookies, cupcakes and brownies on platters and place them on the stand. Set the stand on your dessert buffet. Display shot glasses of milk around the desserts.

24. Utilize specialty cookies for a decorative way to create a favor to place at each place setting at your table. Bake your own cookies or purchase them from a baker. Utilize a design to match your theme. Some examples include a bow tie and gown for a formal affair, a wedding gown and tuxedo for a wedding reception, an olive martini for a cocktail party, baby cookies for a baby shower, Christmas cookies for a Christmas party, cookies for Hanukkah, or cookies designed for a birthday party.

25. Use chocolate to create a name place card for your table place settings. Make the chocolate card out of dark chocolate that has been melted and placed into molds to solidify. You can purchase molds at Michaels Craft Stores or a cooking store. Use rectangular, heart shaped, circular and other shapes to create your place cards. After the chocolate has been removed from the mold place the shapes on a piece of wax paper. Melt white chocolate and place it in a piping bag with a number 5 dot tip attached to the bag and pipe each guests name onto the dark chocolate shapes. Wrap each individual chocolate creation in cellophane and tie off with a ribbon. Place at the top of each guests place setting.

26. **TIP: If you want to learn more about creating candies, working with chocolate or decorating cakes there are books that you can purchase. Michaels Craft Stores has an entire section of cake and candy decorating supplies and books from Wilton Decorating, the premier cake supply company, for home makers interested in creating their own cakes and candies. Michaels Crafts Stores also offer cake decorating classes.**

27. Purchase an inexpensive chocolate fountain for your chocolate fondue or create your own chocolate fondue preparing the fondue in a crock pot using quality chocolate. Set the chocolate fondue next to your fruit display so that your guests can dip the fruit into the chocolate.

> **CHOCOLATE FONDUE**
> **one-half pint whipping cream**
> **one-fourth cup Frambois or Baileys**
> **12 oz milk chocolate or semi sweet chocolate**
> **Melt the chocolate and whipping cream in a double boiler.**
> **Add the Baileys or Frambois and stir.**

28. Dip various fruits in wine cream. Wine cream is a decadent heavy whipping cream flavored with merlot wine. One of the chefs at the Campus Inn Hotel taught me to make this recipe for wine cream.

> **WINE CREAM**
> **one pint heavy whipping cream**
> **one-fourth cup sugar**
> **one-half cup good quality Merlot**
> **Whip the cream, sugar and merlot until thick and peaks form.**
> **Pour into a decorative bowl and serve with skewered fruits.**

29. Chocolate-dipped strawberries make a nice light dessert and go well with champagne as they help to

bring out the flavors of the champagne.

30. Create a chocolate display for a centerpiece to remember. Use truffles and other assorted chocolates and display them in a decorative container in the center of your table.

31. Create a cookie display for a unique dessert centerpiece. Use special platters to display cookies. Place cookies in baskets lined with cloth napkins.

32. For a Christmas cookie display, create a tree made out of cardboard and adhere cookies with icing to the tree. To create the tree make a template of the tree out of paper. Trace and cut two of the templates out of cardboard. To join the two cardboard trees, cut a slit in the bottom half of one of the cardboard trees and cut another slit in the top half of the other card board tree. Insert one into the other sliding the two piece together so that they fit snugly. Cover the tree with icing. Create a platform out of cardboard to glue the tree to with icing. Decorate your tree with cookies. Adhere candies to the tree as well.

33. For a child's party set up a self serve sundae bar for the children to enjoy. Pre-scoop ice cream and store the scoops of ice cream in a punch bowl or other large bowl in your freezer until ready to serve. Place various toppings such as: chocolate shavings, confetti sprinkles, chocolate, caramel and strawberry syrups and whipped cream in bowls. You can use an assortment of crushed candies as well.

34. **TIP: When you set up your sundae bar, place a glow light or a Lexan on the table that you want to set up your sundae bar on, fill the glow light or Lexan with ice and place your punch bowl of ice cream on top of the ice. Arrange bowls, spoons, napkins and your toppings around the ice cream for self service by your guests.**

35. For a unique dessert serve three miniature desserts on one plate.

36. For a fabulous dessert during the Christmas Holidays serve miniature *croquembouche* cakes on dessert plates. You could also have the chef create a *croquembouche* for each table placing the dessert in the center of the table with plates allowing the guests to serve themselves.

37. Display chocolate truffles on small plates of interesting design.

38. Dip strawberries in white chocolate and then dip them in dark chocolate allowing some of the white chocolate to show. Arrange the strawberries on platters to display on your dessert table or place a platter on each dining table.

39. Dip strawberries in white chocolate. Let them dry. Swirl dark chocolate over the white chocolate by dipping a spoon into the melted dark chocolate and swirling it over the white chocolate.

40. Display elevated bowls or platters of cherries, strawberries, and other fruits on your dessert buffet.

41. For a lavish candy display have your caterer or pastry chef create a coach out of chocolate designed to resemble the coach from the Cinderella animation. Use this coach as a centerpiece for chocolate truffles or strawberries painted with chocolate tuxedos and displayed on a mirror. Also use the chocolate coach as a decoration for a dessert platter.

42. Fill clear glass cylinders of various sizes with cut fruits and place them in the center of your buffet. Elevate glass mirrors or platters around your glass cylinders and arrange cubes of cake on the glass mirrors or platters. Fill bowls with sauces such as honey-walnut yogurt into which you can dip the fruits and cubed cake. Arrange food items in the middle of your platters or around the bottom of your

elevated platters. Be sure to have toothpicks available to hold items while dipping into the sauces.

43. Fill cylindrical vases with whole lemons and limes or other whole fruit and top the vases off with platters of petits fours.

44. For a dessert buffet or as a favor for guests to take home, serve monogrammed chocolate truffles to your guests.

45. Create an eclectic design for a dessert station by placing chocolate truffles on sticks, securing them to a base such as a whole melon or arrange them in a vase.

46. For a reception in the fall set up a station with hot apple cider. Utilize a coffee urn or a cambro (a large insulated beverage holder), to keep your beverage hot. Arrange cups around the hot cider and display cinnamon sticks for a garnish, serving donuts with the hot beverage.

47. Display cookies such as meringue cookies or a variety of butter cookies in a box made out of chocolate. Utilize the box of cookies as a centerpiece on your dessert buffet. Have your caterer or pastry chef create the chocolate box.

48. Purchase decorative skewers such as bamboo for your chocolate dipped strawberries.

49. Utilize acrylic trays that have been designed with holes in them to fit paper cones. Fill the paper cones with various snacks such as french-fried sweet potatoes. You can special order these trays from restaurant equipment supply companies. The trays even have a handle attached to the bottom of it so you can hold onto it while you butler pass food items such as waffle cones filled with scoops of homemade ice cream or sorbets.

50. For another take on the dessert station serve miniature cones of ice cream or sorbet. Set deep trays on your dessert station and fill the trays with colored sanding sugar. Stand the tasty treats in the sugar for a unique way of serving ice cream.

51. Serve miniature milk shakes at a child's birthday party.

Ganache is quality chocolate, heavy whipping cream and flavoring such as vanilla or rum.

52. Wrap cookies or ice cream sandwiches in monogrammed parchment paper.

53. At a child's party use acrylic trays with holes in them to display snow cones to butler pass to children.

54. Utilize a heart shaped basket to display heart shaped cookies for a wedding reception or Valentines Day party.

55. For a pretty platter to serve tartlets on, cover the bottom of your platter with doilies. Arrange the tartlets and decorate with a bunch of small flowers or herbs.

56. Utilize paper cupcake liners with a heart design on them for a wedding reception or Valentines Day.

57. Utilize small martini glasses to serve small bites of food.

58. **TIP: Everybody loves chocolate! You can purchase molds to create your own chocolate candies. Choose a design that matches your theme. For a wedding hearts would be appropriate. Place a chocolate candy at each place setting or stuff them in small decorative boxes so that your guests can carry them home when they leave the reception. Remember you can purchase candy making supplies from Wilton Decorating at Michaels Craft stores. They also supply directions on how to make candies.**

59. Serve specialty ice creams such as paletas.
60. Fill monogrammed cornucopias with candy as take home treats for a child's party.
61. Create a chocolate or raspberry coulis heart design around the perimeter of your dessert plates. Pour the raspberry coulis or chocolate in a pastry bag with a # 5 dot tip attached. Put drops of raspberry coulis or melted chocolate at intervals around the perimeter of your dessert plate. Use the tip of a utility knife or toothpick and slowly drag it through the coulis or chocolate starting at the top of one of the drops continuing through each drop until you have circled the entire plate with hearts.
62. Purchase fortune cookies with special messages in them. You can buy fortune cookies with messages that contain various themes such as a Valentines Day theme with words of love. Decorate your fortune cookies with dark or white chocolate and nuts or nonpareils to add a special touch.
63. Use cookies as name place cards. Create the cookie shape that you desire; pipe each guest's name onto the cookie with icing and then you can wrap in cellophane for presentation.
64. For a child's birthday party set up a candy station with various bowls or jars of candy. Place monogrammed bags on the station for the children to fill and take home with them.
65. A great way to serve dessert to children and entertain them at the same time is to set up a dessert bar with cupcakes and various decorative candies. Let them create their own signature cupcakes.
66. Glass shot glasses are a great way to serve light desserts such as a mousse to your guests. Arrange them on trays or arrange them directly onto your dessert table.
67. For a unique way to serve cupcakes, place the iced cupcake on a stick. Display cupcakes inserted into a Styrofoam disk or fill a bowl with colored sugar and stand the cupcakes upright.
68. Display tiny desserts such as assorted mousses on a solid cupcake tier. Stack cake stands one atop the other in place of the cupcake tier. Place the mousse in small plastic cups. The cups can be purchased at restaurant supply companies. Use the stands to display petits fours. Place your displays on your dessert station.
69. Place individual chocolate fondue pots in the center of each dining table. Serve a platter consisting of dried fruits and cake bites.
70. Serve heart shaped cookies that have been covered in colored sugars to match your color scheme.

***Petit four* means "small oven" in French.**

70. For a unique dessert serve three different mousses in shot glasses on a plate.
71. Create or buy a template with the initials of the bride and groom. Place the template off center on your dessert plate and sprinkle powdered sugar or cocoa powder to fill in the design. Gently lift the template off of the plate. Arrange a slice of wedding cake next to the design.
72. Lay a paper doily on top of your dessert plate sprinkle powdered sugar or cocoa powder over the doily to fill in the design. Gently lift the doily off of the plate. Lay your dessert on top of the design.

Here is my recipe for Bananas Foster. This is how I made it when we served it at the hotel. I would make enough of the Bananas Foster to serve six people at a time since we had to work quickly in order to prevent a line from forming at the dessert station and keep guests from waiting long periods of time.

BANANAS FOSTER

½ cup of butter cut into pieces
1 and 1/3 cup brown sugar
½ cup dark rum
¼ cup banana liqueur
1 teaspoon cinnamon
3 bananas sliced into coins

Melt the butter in a sauté pan over a burner. Add the brown sugar, banana liqueur and cinnamon and dissolve cooking until bubbly. Add the slices of banana and cook for one to two minutes until bananas are tender and slightly brown. Add the dark rum to the pan and slightly tilt the pan so that the flame ignites the dark rum allowing the alcohol to burn off of the dessert. Place a small amount of the banana mixture into each of six bowls and top with a scoop of vanilla ice cream.

5: WEDDING CAKES
"Let them eat cake." Marie Antoinette

What You Need to Know

This section on wedding cakes lists ideas for displaying wedding cakes as well as decoration and alternatives to the traditional wedding cake. You want to use your imagination, be creative with your cake design as well as display. Use color as a cue or items that translate the theme of your special event such as a repeating pattern, motif or linen detail in lace or printed cloth. Let your style be your guide. Work with your baker to create a beautiful wedding cake for your reception.

When planning your wedding reception search for a pastry chef to create your dream wedding cake six to eight months in advance. You need to make sure that you allow yourself plenty of time to find the bakery that is right for you. You want to visit several shops and sample cake flavors to determine how you want your cake to taste. Bring pictures, color samples, flowers or any other items that will express the way you want your design to look. This will help the chef create a wedding cake that mirrors the style of the bride.

EVENTS YOU DESIGN

The bakery needs to know what date you are planning on getting married so that they can confirm that this date is available. Inform them of the number of guests in attendance, the time of your event and the location. Be sure to find out if there will be a delivery and setup fee. Create a list of questions specific to your needs and take it with you when you interview pastry chefs.

SAMPLE QUESTIONS FOR THE PASTRY CHEF
1. What information do you need to know about the bride and groom in order to design the perfect wedding cake?
2. How many tiers do I need to feed the number of guests invited?
3. What is the cost per slice?
4. Is my chosen date available?
5. Will you personally deliver and set up my cake?
6. Is there a fee for delivery?
7. Will you setup a tasting so I can sample cake flavors?
8. Can you show me pictures of cakes you have designed?
9. Can you provide me with references?

INFORMATION TO BE INCLUDED ON A CONTRACT PROVIDED BY THE BAKERY
1. The company name, address and phone number.
2. Day and date of the event
3. Name and address of the event site.
4. Start time of the event and expected delivery time.
5. Name of on site contact person.
6. Type of event, for example, wedding, birthday etc.
7. The cost per slice.
8. Detailed information: number of tiers, layers, slices, cake flavor, decoration and colors.
9. Deposits paid.
10. Amounts due.
11. Cancellation date.
12. Delivery costs.
13. Available insurance for any damage to the cake.
14. Dated and signed by client and pastry chef.

Make sure that the person who cuts your cake knows the proper way to cut a wedding cake. Be sure to have wait staff serve cake to your guests. If cake is not passed often times guests do not help themselves and cake is left behind. If you are serving a buffet dinner be sure to cut the cake before dinner is served so that guests can be served cake as soon as they finish their meal. Also be sure to send any left over cake home with your guests utilizing to-go cake boxes monogrammed with essential information such as the bride's and groom's initials and date of the event. Use the list of ideas below to help you style your wedding cake, display it with elegance or help to create an alternative to the traditional wedding cake. Take any of these ideas along with you when you discuss your cake with a baker, event decorator, the caterer or event planner so that they can help you dream up an enchanting wedding cake.

WEDDING CAKES: A List of 129 Ideas for Attractively Decorating and Displaying Them Couverture is quality coating chocolate.

1. Carry your theme into your wedding cake design by using elements such as color, texture or a repeating design in the decorating of your wedding cake.
2. Utilize elements of your wedding dress such as a bow or a brooch in your wedding cake design.
3. **TIP: Set up a separate table to hold cake plates, salad forks and napkins for your wedding cake service. Keep the cake cutting tools handy on this table and also supply a pitcher of hot water to expedite the cake cutting process. Be sure to cover the pitcher that contains the hot water with a cloth napkin for a nice presentation. Also have damp cloths available for the bride and groom to wipe their hands with after the cake cutting ceremony is finished.**
4. **TIP: After the bride and groom cut the wedding cake and feed each other they will have the need to wipe their hands on a wet cloth to remove the excess wedding cake from their fingers. Take two cloth napkins and fold each one into an artichoke fold. To learn how to make different napkin folds go to the internet and Google napkin folds and you will find directions on how to design a variety of folds. Place each artichoke fold onto a salad plate. Take two additional napkins and fold the sides in about an inch and then fold into thirds and roll tightly like an egg roll. Place each of these rolls into separate small porcelain gratin dishes. Set each gratin dish on top of one of the artichoke folded napkins and reserve them for the cake cutting, placing them on the table with the cake plates. Wet the napkins just before the wedding cake is to be cut.**
5. Be sure to ask your lighting specialist to highlight your wedding cake with pin spotlighting.
6. **TIP: When you talk to bakers about designing your wedding cake ask to see pictures of their work. Have them create a simple sketch of what your cake will look like. Bring samples of fabric swatches or invitations and so on so the baker can see what your wedding colors look like and patterns that you might like them to incorporate into the design of your cake. Be sure to ask for flavor samples so you can determine how you want your cake to taste.**
7. Arrange frosted grapes or other whole fruits around your wedding cake.

> **To frost dip cluster of grapes or fruit in egg whites.**
> **Let them dry briefly and then dip them into sugar drying them completely.**

8. Utilize a small round cocktail table for a cake display. Cover and skirt the table. Elevate the cake by using a glass rack covered with a cloth. Be sure to fluff around the elevation with sheer fabric and arrange flowers of the bride's choice in the fluff.

9. For a simple elevation for your wedding cake utilize glass blocks to elevate the cake. Arrange glass votives to highlight the cake and cast a shine on the glass blocks. Decorative glass blocks can be purchased from a restaurant supply company.

10. Use click lights to light up a glass base positioned underneath your wedding cake. The click lights will adhere to the inside of your glass base. Use a bowl with a flat bottom for your base and adhere the click lights to the inside bottom of the glass bowl. Activate the lights by clicking them on and then invert the base onto the middle of the cake table. Perch your cake on top of the base.

11. Have your baker design a wedding cake that is white and chocolate at the same time. One half of the cake will be white with white icing to represent the bride and the other half chocolate with chocolate icing to represent the groom.

12. Have your baker design a groom's cake based on the groom's hobby or favorite sports team.

13. Utilize a dummy wedding cake to display decorated cupcakes as an alternative to a wedding cake. A dummy cake can be made out of styrofoam and covered with rolled fondant. Decorate the tiered dummy cake as desired and arrange cupcakes on each tier.

14. The wedding cake should always be the focal point. Create a unique backdrop for a wedding cake that has very little embellishment. Arrange willow branches that have been entwined with fresh flowers behind the wedding cake. This is an elegant way to showcase a simple wedding cake.

15. As a wedding cake alternative, have your baker prepare individual wedding cakes for each guest to enjoy. Decorate your miniature wedding cakes with icing flowers and ribbon to create elegance.

16. Another unique way to let them eat cake at your wedding reception is to have your baker create individual heart shaped cakes. Have the initials of the bride and groom monogrammed on top of the cakes or sayings such as SWEETHEART, LOVE or BE MINE.

17. For a sweet alternative to the traditional wedding cake have your baker create individual cherry pies to serve your guests as a special treat. Make sure that the baker cuts a heart design into the top layer of the pastry crust as a symbol of love revealing the luscious cherry filling.

19. For an alternative to the groom's cake have your baker create cupcakes and decorate them with a tuxedo design. Stack silver cake stands of three different sizes on top of each other placing the largest on the bottom and the smallest on top to create a tiered effect. Arrange the cupcakes on the cake stands. You can purchase plastic tiered cupcake holders from Michaels Craft stores or at Wilton.com.

20. For a twist on the traditional wedding cake ask your baker to prepare a Napoleon or other dessert for your guests to enjoy.

If you bake a cake utilizing a cake mix remember that two cake mixes serve 30 people.

21. As an accompaniment to your wedding cake serve strawberries that have been dipped in milk, dark and white chocolate.

22. Set up a candy station at your wedding reception. Display a multitude of candies or choose candies

that coordinate with your color scheme. Have Chinese to-go boxes or cellophane or wax bags with initials and date of event stamped on them. Your guests can take home the sweets as a souvenir.

23. Serve petits fours with the initials of the bride and groom monogrammed in chocolate on each one.

24. Fresh flowers look great on a wedding cake. Try something different by placing the wedding cake on a base of fresh flowers. Your florist can create this base for you. When you place the cake on the base, be sure the cake is sitting on a plastic tray to prevent the bottom layer of the cake from getting wet. You could also create a disk of flowers to place in between each layer of cake.

25. Another beautiful way of displaying your wedding cake is to have the florist design a tabletop out of flowers to place over the top of your skirted cake table.

26. For a wedding reception have your baker create heart shaped cookies with a picture of the bride and groom on the cookie.

27. As a backdrop for your wedding cake table, hang sheer fabric and swags in colors to match your color scheme behind the cake table. Light the backdrop with colored lighting to match your color scheme.

28. For another great backdrop for your wedding cake consider using potted plants. Palm trees, ferns or potted flowers make a great display behind a cake table. Light the plants with neutral colors.

29. When covering a cake table utilize fabric that drapes to the floor and can be shaped or fluffed at the bottom. Pin a swag of material around the top edge of the cake table for an inexpensive, elegant look.

30. For an inexpensive way to dress up your wedding cake have the bridesmaids place their bouquets around the base of the cake.

31. To create a gazebo effect for your wedding cake have your florist strategically place columns that have been wrapped with fresh flowers around the perimeter of your wedding cake table.

32. Have your florist hang garlands of flowers around the perimeter of the wedding cake table.

33. Display your wedding cake on a square table instead of a round table.

34. For a creative way to showcase the wedding cake hang a portrait of the bride and groom in back of the wedding cake.

35. Have your baker create cupcakes for your wedding reception and serve them in place of a cake. Frost the cupcakes and insert a flag that is monogrammed with the initials of the bride and groom.

36. Place your wedding cake on a stand that will raise the cake approximately seven inches off of the cake table. Arrange photographs of the bride and groom around the cake stand.

37. Have your baker create individual bundt cakes instead of a wedding cake. Ice and arrange flowers in the center of each bundt cake and place a cake in the center of each dining table.

38. Have your baker shape the initials of the bride and groom out of wire and decorate them with gum paste flowers for a personalized cake topper.

39. Create a wedding cake topper out of wire shaped as two hearts and decorate the wire hearts with gum paste flowers.

40. Drape sheer swags of pastel colors on the wall behind your wedding cake to create a romantic effect for your wedding cake setting. Use fabrics such as lamé, or tulle adhering the fabric to the walls with

tacks. Also incorporate flowers into the design by placing tiny bouquets throughout the swags.

41. **TIP: To save money on the cost of a wedding cake have your baker create a small wedding cake for the bride and groom to cut. Utilize sheet cakes to serve your guests. Have the wait staff cut the sheet cakes and place pieces of cake on salad plates and serve to your guests.**

42. Have a sheet cake cut into slices and pre-placed. Inscribe the bride's and groom's initials on the plate with chocolate.

43. Have your baker monogram your wedding cake. You do not have to decorate your cake with flowers to create a stunning effect.

44. Have your baker paint flowers or other designs on your wedding cake with edible paints.

45. To create a stunning wedding cake table use a petticoat designed specifically to cover a cake table. Linen rental companies should be able to supply you with a petticoat.

46. You can make your own petticoat with layers of netting for fullness, a layer of soft tulle and a top layer of white taffeta. Attach a wide satin ribbon around the top edge of the layers to hold all the layers of fabric together. Cover your cake table with a white tablecloth. Pin the petticoat to the tablecloth utilizing white button tea pins. Hang a small swag of flowers on the front side of the cake table. Use a ribbon that has pearls sewn into it or a ribbon in a color to match your color scheme.

47. Use a square glass and metal decorative wall shelf to display your wedding cake.

48. Have your baker create a dessert alternative to a traditional wedding cake by baking hearts, flowers, round or square cookies in three different sizes. Ice the cookies and stack them according to size, three layers high and decorate them like you would a wedding cake.

49. Utilize small decorated to-go boxes with handles to send sliced wedding cake with the bride and groom as they leave the reception to go on their honeymoon.

50. Have your florist create a dummy cake for your wedding reception using oasis and fresh flowers.

51. Serve an alternate dessert in place of the traditional wedding cake.

52. Another way to highlight your cake is to place glass votive candles around the base of your cake. This is an inexpensive way to add elegance to your wedding cake display.

53. Have your baker create a spectacular wedding cake by decorating the cake with written messages that convey your feelings on this special day.

54. For an alternative to wedding cake have your baker create cakes to place in the center of each table for self-service by your guests.

55. Create a special sign that has the bride's and groom's names inscribed upon it for a cake topper.

56. For a beautiful cake table, utilize a 60-inch round or cocktail table; cover the table with a white cloth. Hang swags of greenery around the top edge of the table. Pin a bouquet of flowers at the top edge of each swag.

57. Utilize swags of fresh flowers to drape around the top of your cake table.

58. Decorate a wedding cake by placing spun sugar in pastel colors around the bottom of the cake to create an ethereal effect.

59. Create a cake stand for the groom's cake by making a wooden box six inches in height to accommodate the circumference of the cake. Cover the box in white fabric and use black fabric to create a la-

pel and bow tie, giving the box the look of a tux.

60. Have your baker decorate individual brownies to look like a wedding dress or a tuxedo.

61. Have your pastry chef or caterer decorate strawberries with milk chocolate and white chocolate so that they look like a bride's dress or a tuxedo.

62. Cover your cake table with a white tablecloth. Place tiny white lights on the top of your cake table ensuring that they are spread across the entire tabletop. Be sure to have the cord and prong hang from the backside of the table so that they will not be seen. Cover the lights with sheer gold fabric allowing the fabric to extend over the sides of the table or fluff the fabric directly on the lights.

63. If your venue has a balcony in the area where your wedding reception is to take place, stage the cake on the balcony.

64. If your venue has a stage in the area where your reception is to take place, put the cake on stage.

65. If a stage is not available create one just for the wedding cake.

66. **TIP: For a unique way to display the cake table place it behind the head table. Arrange two six -foot tables along with a quarter round at angles insuring that they are joined as one by placing the quarter round in between each of the two six-foot tables. Make sure that tables are set up in the front of the room so that the bride and groom and wedding party can be seen by the guests. Also make sure that the point that is created when the two six-foot tables are joined with the quarter round faces the guests tables. Place the cake table in back of this table. Remember to arrange chairs on the back side of the head table. See pages 102-103 on floor diagrams for other ideas on how to set up the head table in conjunction with the cake table.**

67. Serve wedding cookies that have been decorated with the bride's and groom's initials.

68. As an accompaniment to cake serve strawberries or chocolate covered strawberries.

69. For a dessert created just for your wedding reception have the pastry chef decorate slices of cake with two chocolate hearts nestled on top. Use white and milk chocolate hearts.

70. For a wedding reception serve each guest a plated slice of cake with the initials or names of the bride and groom on each slice.

71. Place two small satellite cakes, along side of your tiered wedding cake, with the initials of the bride atop one and the groom atop the other. You could also place the initials of the bride and groom both atop of each satellite cake.

72. Hang many paper lanterns above your cake.

73. Serve the bride and groom bite-sized cakes.

74. For a unique way to display your wedding cake attach four long pieces of sheer fabric to the ceiling above your cake table, making sure that the fabric is long enough to reach the table. Attach the sheer fabric to the table at four different points. Create bows and attach at each of the four points on the table. You might also add flowers to the sheer fabric.

75. **TIP: Serving cupcakes, for example, as opposed to a wedding cake, can save you money. Be sure to serve a variety of flavors: lemon, chocolate, vanilla and strawberry, for example.**

76. Save money on dessert by placing a basket or platter of cookies on each dinner table.

77. Create a dummy wedding cake. Place party favors such as small bags of candies or cellophane

wrapped cookies on each tier of the dummy cake.

78. Cupcakes replace your wedding cake; add whimsy by placing candy hearts embossed with messages such as; I LOVE YOU, BE MINE or SWEETHEART in the icing. Place chocolate hearts monogrammed with the bride's and groom's initial as another way to decorate cupcakes.

79. Decorate bite-sized cakes for the bride and groom to enjoy!

80. Serve cookies shaped in the initials of the bride and groom.

81. Create a cake table utilizing hollow Plexiglass squares approximately two and one-half feet tall. Fill them with flowers. Set your cake board on top of the hollow Plexiglass squares.

82. Display your wedding cake on a tall pedestal that sits in the center of the bride's and groom's table.

83. To create a stunning wedding cake display hang many lanterns of the same or varying colors, directly above your cake, casting a glow onto the cake. Incorporate sheer swags of fabric along with the lanterns by hanging the swags from the ceiling.

84. For a modern touch on a cake display, sprinkle rose petals around the perimeter of the cake. Display messages, such as, "I LOVE YOU" or "JUST MARRIED" made out of colorful letters.

85. Light your wedding cake by hanging crystals from the ceiling directly above your cake. Create a square frame approximately two-feet x two-feet. Attach it directly to the ceiling above where your cake table will set. Hang the long strands of crystals and some glass votives from inside of the square frame.

86. Let them eat cake in style. Place your wedding cake on a round cake table that has been clothed. Set a clothed six-foot table in back of the round table. Place tree branches in a square pot that has been filled with cement, rocks, dirt or sand. Hang votives from the tree branches. Arrange cake plates, napkins and dessert forks around the potted tree.

87. **TIP: Have six-foot tables arranged side by side in the front of your room. Three people can sit comfortably at each six-foot table, so use this as a guide to determine how many tables you need. This will be the head table for the bride, groom and wedding party. Place the cake table approximately four feet in front of this arrangement.**

88. Set your wedding cake stand on top of a lace doily or a piece of fabric in a pattern or color to match your theme.

89. Set up a cupcake tree by placing cake stands of various sizes one on top of the other. Place the largest on the bottom and the smallest on the top. Place a small cake at the top and cupcakes on the bottom tiers.

90. Make your table part of the overall cake design. Match the table linen to the icing color, utilize table linen with a floral design to match your flowers, remember to be creative!

91. Place your wedding cake in the center of a square design alternating votive candles and flowers.

92. Place your cake in the center of a circle design alternating votive candles and rose petals.

93. Set up your cake table and cover with a cloth. Hang a swag created by cutting out three cards of the same size and joining them together with ribbons tied into bows that match your color scheme. Place messages on the cards such as, I LOVE YOU! Put the names of the bride and groom on the cards. Be sure to attach ribbons on each of the two end cards so that you can hang the swag to the front of

your cake table.

94. Follow the theme of your cake design onto the cake board that the cake rests on by incorporating design elements from your event into the cake board.

95. Drape your cake table in a white netting tent.

96. Place two ficus trees on either side of the wedding cake table. Hang candles and flowers that match the theme from the branches of the trees. This is a great way to highlight your cake.

97. For an updated cake table, cover the table with a printed cloth such as polka dots and place a solid cover overlay to match on top.

98. Serve miniature wedding cakes in lieu of a wedding cake. Place the initials of the last name of the newly married couple on top of each cake.

99. Utilize a mirror to cover your cake tabletop.

100. Be sure to display to-go boxes along side of your cupcake tree.

101. Showcase your cake with arches of balloons.

102. Use a crescent table to display your wedding cake. Place the table against a wall in a prominent location and place a ficus tree behind the table. String lights onto the ficus tree.

103. Place the wedding cake table close to the wall and use Gobos to project the initials and any pertinent information above the cake on the wall. According to Kinetic Lighting a Gobo is a template that can be inserted into certain lighting fixtures to project an image.

104. Use a square table to house a square wedding cake.

105. Cover the wedding cake table with sheer fabric and pin swags of fabric such as netting to the top edges of the table. Set up lights beneath the table to light the cake from beneath.

SUGGESTED QUOTE: This day I will marry my best friend, the one I laugh with, live for, love!

106. Drape your cake plate with lace.

107. Cover a tallboy table with sheer fabric and display your wedding cake on top.

108. Sprinkle confetti hearts around your cake display.

109. Create a design around your cake display by arranging confetti in the pattern of a heart or hearts on the tabletop.

110. Use four large square vases as a base to display your wedding cake. Place four fresh cut flowers on your tabletop spacing them evenly in a square design. Place a clear square vase over each flower. Be sure that each vase is positioned so that they can hold the cake board securely.

111. Also use four tall cylindrical vases filled with flowers as the base for your cake display.

112. Cover the elevation that will hold your cake in a fabric to match your icing color.

113. Place a fancy mirror on the wall behind your wedding cake. Arrange votives around your cake.

114. Set your wedding cake on a cake board that is larger than your wedding cake. Lay the initials of the bride and groom next to the cake on the cake board.

115. Place a potted tree behind your cake table. Hang long strands of crystals and candles from the branches.

116. Hang strands of tiny white lights directly above your wedding cake.

117. Hang swags and round clusters of flowers directly above your wedding cake.

118. TIP: The last thing you eat is the cake so it has to be good.

119. Create an awning to stage your wedding cake ceremony under by creating a frame out of wood and covering it with sheer fabric. Place the cake table under this awning. Arrange a pedestal on either side of the awning. Place a flower arrangement on each pedestal.

120. Center a column in the front of your room. Place a cocktail table on either side of the column and cloth them. Set your wedding cake on one table and cupcakes on the other. You might place flowers on the top of the column.

121. If you use a cupcake tree, place a flower arrangement on the top in lieu of a small cake.

122. Use words such as: LOVE, I DO and MARRIED, for a cake topper. Have your florist create the design out of flowers. Have your pastry chef create them out of icing or gum paste flowers. Create the words of your choice out of cardboard paper. Be creative.

123. Hang words such as: I DO, I LOVE YOU, and MARRIED above your wedding cake utilizing decorative ribbon. Create the words from cardboard with glitter, fabric or paper with patterns on it. Use two types of paper, one in a solid color the other with a pattern.

124. Create a petticoat out of feathers to cover your cake table.

125. Utilize a petticoat covered in sequins for your cake table.

126. Place your cake in front of a wall of water.

127. Place your wedding cake on a covered cocktail table. Stage a board that stands taller than the cake in back of the table. Paint or cover the board to match your color scheme. Place a band of ribbon down the middle of the board. Instead of a band of ribbon place a line of pictures of the bride and groom down the center of the board.

128. Use a petticoat covered with sequins for your cake table.

129. Have your lighting person direct sayings such as, I LOVE YOU, ENDLESS LOVE and I DO on the wall behind the wedding cake.

CUTTING THE WEDDING CAKE

If you have never cut a wedding cake it is not hard to do. Remember to have all of the necessary tools at hand. You will need a knife and cake spatula as well as a pitcher of hot water and a towel to clean the knife with. Be sure to have cake plates next to or on the cake table and also have dessert forks and napkins ready to place along side of the cake slices.

    The first step in cutting the cake is to remove the top layer placing it into a box for the bride and groom to take home to enjoy on their first anniversary. Now you are ready to cut the second layer. Be sure to remove any fresh flowers or other non-edible decorations. Once this step has been completed you are ready to make the first cut. Start by cutting a circle in the center of the cake. Once the circle is complete cut slices that extend from the outside of the circle to the edge of the cake, keeping the inner circle intact. Once you have cut slices around the outside edge of your circle and placed those slices on cake plates you are ready to cut the inner circle in slices. Continue with the next layer and so on in the same manner as before. You need to gauge the size of each slice based on the number of guests in attendance.

6: BEVERAGES

The Greeks placed a wreath of ivy around their wine bottle.
They believed this would prevent them from getting drunk..

How to Choose Beverages and Design a Bar to Fit Your Party Needs

Let's celebrate with a toast to, "Health, wealth, love and time to enjoy them all." When we think of raising a glass to make a toast most of us think of champagne. A toast does not have to be made with champagne anymore. There are many options for beverage selection, champagne is not the only dazzling sparkling drink at the party. Create your own signature drink for your guests to imbibe as they reflect on your time of celebration. Choose a drink that reflects the rest of your meal. Have a full-service bar that allows your guests to choose what they would like to partake of during your toast. There are many options and lots of creative ways to serve both alcoholic spirits and non-alcoholic beverages.

You have options when it comes to bars. There are two types of bars, one is a full-service bar and the other is a satellite bar. The full-service bar requires a bartender while the satellite bar can be self service. The full-service bar has a variety of liquors and mixers. The satellite bar will have beers, wine, soft drinks and bottled water. The satellite bar requires very little skill while the full-service bar requires the skills of a bartender in order to create cocktails of varying degrees. The satellite bar may also have a signature drink that has been pre-mixed and merely needs to be poured into a glass to be enjoyed. If you have a large number of guests in attendance, it is a good idea to have a full-service bar along with a satellite bar. The satellite bar will free up the line so that guests that wish to sip on a glass of wine, beer or soda can quickly retrieve their beverage while those who prefer a cocktail can utilize the full-service bar.

When it comes to setting up a basic full-service bar you need certain ingredients. There is no set rule as to how much alcohol to purchase for a bar. It really does come down to an estimation. If you know what your guests like to drink this will help you in making your determination. The menu and even the time of year play a role in what beverages you will serve. As a general rule, white wines seem to be a little more popular than reds especially in the summer when it is hot outside, but red wine is gaining in popularity because of its purported health benefits. I have found from experience that on the average vodka and whisky such as Jack Daniels seem to be served most often and you might want to have extra of those two on hand. From a banquet standpoint experience is the best way to determine what beverages to serve. You can always look back at a group's past history to see what they consumed most. Be sure to consult with the professionals when deciding on beverage choices. The information below will give you some numbers that will help you when determining how much alcohol to purchase for your bar.

Here is a basic formula for determining how many drinks you will serve at your event. Four drinks per person is an average number used when determining how many drinks and the approximate amounts of alcohol to purchase. You might also consider the type of guests attending your event. Are they heavy or light drinkers? And also keep in mind the length of time the party runs. Two other factors to consider would be the amount of money budgeted for alcohol and guest safety.

4 drinks per guest x the number of guests = the number of drinks served

The amount of liquor and wine to purchase for a party in your home is subjective. Even if we use our formula from above we don't know what drinks will be most popular. Will your guests prefer cocktails to wine? That is a bit of a dilemma. So how do you know how much wine or alcohol to purchase? Basically an educated guess is the determining factor. In a hotel setting they keep a par stock level of beverages on hand for all of their catered events. On a bar they base the amount of liquor, wine and beer stocked simply by estimating the amounts consumed from a group's previous event. I have found that vodka and Jack Daniels seem to be most popular. In a hotel setting they can always restock a particular beverage if they need to do so and that is the job of the bar back. Because they keep a par stock level in the liquor cage they are able to replenish at a moment's notice. For parties in your home you may wish to keep extra liquor or wine on hand for future use.

Below are the formulas for determining how many drinks you will pour from a bottle of wine or liquor.

750-ml bottle of wine pours 5 six-ounce glasses. This is a basic bartender's formula.
750-ml bottle of liquor pours 15 cocktails, that is if you stick to a 50-ml shot per drink.
A basic calculation would be 750-ml divided by 50-ml equals 15 drinks.

Let the sales person at your local liquor store help you determine how much alcohol to purchase for your party. If your event is to be held at a hotel or other establishment that has a license to sell alcohol they will guide you with your choices.

Below is listed a general guideline for basic ingredients needed to complete a full-service bar.

Alcohol
Start with these liquors and you can always add any others that you enjoy such as Baileys Irish Cream or Kahlua. Liquors: vodka, gin, rum, tequila, whisky, bourbon, scotch, sweet vermouth, dry vermouth and triple sec. Serve wines such as Merlot or Cabernet, Chardonnay or Sauvignon Blanc and White Zinfandel. Serve an assortment of domestic, import and nonalcoholic beers. Be sure to have plenty of alcohol on hand. Remember it is a very important part of the festivities and you do not want to run out.

Mixers
Have mixers on hand such as Coke, Diet Coke, Sprite, ginger ale, tonic water, soda water, orange juice, cranberry juice, grapefruit juice, bottled water, Bloody Mary mix, margarita mix, sour mix, Rose's lime juice, grenadine, and angostura bitters.

Garnishes

Garnishes include: rimming sugar, rimming salt, lime wedges, lemon wedges, lemon peel, maraschino cherries, olives and pearl onions. Various drinks require different garnishes.

Glassware

The basic glassware is also necessary to set up a full-service bar properly. Glassware includes rock and wine glasses. To make the proper martini you want a martini glass and some drinks require a Collins glass which is a tall glass.

Tools

Tools that will be required include: cork screw, utility knife, small cutting board for cutting garnishes, descended bar spoon or muddler for bruising fresh herbs to release essence, shaker, Hawthorn strainer, ice scoop and bottle opener. Also have bar cloths available for any spills that need to be cleaned up.

Ice

Be sure to have enough ice to cover Lexans of beer and wine as well as for drinks that require ice. Be sure to ice down beer and wines ahead of time so that they will be sufficiently chilled.

These are the essentials for making the basic drinks. You can create many an intoxicating drink with these primary elements and please even the most selective drinkers. If you are not familiar with the chemistry of mixing alcoholic beverages then you should consider hiring a bartender especially if your party consists of a large gathering of people.

For a small group consider purchasing a book of cocktail recipes and strategically place it on your bar as a quick reference to anyone needing assistance in concocting his or her own beverages. Be sure to place a menu on your bar so that guests can see what beverages are available and if you have a signature drink place the recipe on your bar. If you choose to hire a bartender there are companies that out source staff and they can supply a professional bartender at a rate of about $15.00 to $25.00 per hour. If your bartenders are exceptionally good please allow them to accept tips. The rate that you are paying for bartending services is not necessarily the rate given them by the company. Remember that the staffing company has to make money as well as the bartenders.

If you are interested in gaining more information on basic bartending or instructions on how to set up a bar, talk with the staff at your local liquor store. The staff is knowledgeable and more than happy to give you any advice necessary to the setup and service of your bar. If you want to learn more about pairing wines with food or wine in general, many restaurants offer a wine tasting at a reasonable price and they are pairing wines with foods. This is an affordable way to learn and relatively inexpensive. You can also hire a sommelier to come to your home and teach you the basics on wine. The sommelier is an expert on the subject of wine. Also read books on the subject.

TIP: Utilize one beverage bar per 100 guests to expedite the flow of traffic through your bar.

"In Vino Veritas (In wine there is truth)."

Use imagination to create the perfect bar. If you do not wish to have a full-service bar have a satellite bar with a special drink offering, such as sangria, garnished with strawberries and cherries for a festive beverage. Consider serving your favorite drink in place of a full-service or satellite bar but be sure to offer sodas and bottled water for those who prefer not to drink alcoholic beverages. The list below is designed to give you ideas for decorating bars and bar setup.

BEVERAGES: A List of 82 Ideas for Bars, Drinks and Ways for Attractively Displaying Them

1. Decorate your bar with fruits.
2. Place bowls of nuts on your bar.
3. Place a cheese and cracker display on your bar.
4. Add fruit to your cheese and cracker display.
5. For specialty drinks utilize different fruits and veggies as garnishes such as skewered melon balls for a Midori Melon Daiquiri.
6. **TIP: To chill white wine or champagne faster place the bottle in ice and swirl it around using the neck of the bottle in between the palms of your hands.**
7. **TIP: Create a menu for your bar listing the liquor, beer, wine and any soft drinks available. Set the framed menu on top so that your guests can view the menu when they approach the bar. This makes it easier for the guest to determine what they would like to drink and will help the line at your bar to move more quickly.**

TIP: Here is a quick and easy way to make lemon twists to garnish your cocktails. First soak the lemon in hot water to loosen the skin from the pulp. Cut the ends off of the lemon. If you have a grapefruit cutter use it to hollow out the lemon by cutting around the interior of the rind. If not use a small utility knife. Cut the shell into strips, and place a toothpick into each one until you are ready to use them.

8. Place the name of the company or bride's and groom's initials at the top of your menu. For a wedding reception add hearts or another romantic theme to the menu. For a company event incorporate the company logo into the menu graphics.

BAR SIGN EXAMPLE

WELCOME to PAUL and TERESA'S WINE BAR
WINES for YOUR ENJOYMENT!

Cabernet Sauvignon	**Chardonnay**
Merlot	**Pinot Blanc**
Pinot Noir	**Riesling**
Syrah	**Sauvignon Blanc**
Tempranillo	**Gewurztraminer**

If you like, add descriptions of wines. Use this example for a rum, tequila or vodka bar as well.

EXAMPLE BAR LIST
AVAILABLE AT THE BAR FOR YOUR ENJOYMENT

Absolute Vodka	Kentucky Bourbon	Miller and Miller Light beers
Beefeater Gin	Cutty Sark	Coke, Diet Coke, Sprite
Cuervo Gold Tequila	Kendall Jackson Chardonnay	Bottled Water
Bacardi Rum	Black Stone Merlot	Still and Sparkling
Jack Daniels	Fetzer White Zinfandel	

---

9. If you have a specialty drink, such as sangria, be sure to post the recipe. Create a recipe card to display and one for your guests to take home as a party favor by attaching the recipe card to a bottle of the red wine used in the drink. Be sure to include any party info and a thank you to your guests for attending your party. You could also have a picture of the bride and groom on the recipe card.
Sangria is a red wine punch. Choose a red wine that will taste good on its own and not the cheapest wine on the shelf. Be sure to display the sangria in a pitcher with a strainer and pour into wine glasses garnishing your drink with slices of orange, apple and a cherry for decoration.
   Here is a basic sangria recipe:

SANGRIA
18 oz Merlot or Rioja (red from Spain)
6 oz orange juice
6 oz triple sec
6 oz sparkling water
1 orange, apple sliced and ½ c cherries
Ice, Fruit for garnishing

Mix the red wine, orange juice, triple sec, sliced fruit and cherries in a pitcher, cover tightly, and place in the refrigerator over night so that flavors have a chance to infuse. When ready to serve the beverage remove it from the refrigerator, strain, add the ice and pour into wine glasses or collins glasses and garnish.

"Agony of the leaves" in Spain refers to this process: Place tea leaves in the bottom of a cup. Pour hot water on top of them to release all of the flavors from the tea leaves.

10. TIP: Be sure to place bars in areas with plenty of space to approach them.
11. TIP: To avoid long lines at the bar have wait staff butler pass wine to your guests. They might also butler pass beer, water and sodas.
12. TIP: If you are not familiar with wine, while selecting wines for a party talk with the sales person at your wine shop and get suggestions from them. They can help you make good choices without putting a huge dent in your wallet.
13. Create a signature drink for your special event. For a wedding reception a cosmopolitan which combines vodka with a splash of Cointreau, cranberry juice and Rose's lime juice, makes a great signature drink. The bellini, which is a combination of peach juice and champagne, is another great signa-

ture drink. Choose your favorite drink or create a drink just for your special occasion.

14. Design a vodka bar for your event. You can create a variety of drinks with vodka and mixers.
15. For a makeshift bar, use a sink to ice down beers, wine and sodas for self-service. Place glassware, bowl of ice, ice scoop, cocktail napkins, corkscrew, bottle opener on the counter next to the sink.

"Beer is made by men, wine by God!" Martin Luther

16. Serve cocktails that are festively decorated with umbrellas or flags with initials or sayings on them.
17. Serve his and hers signature drinks by allowing the bride and groom to create drinks to showcase their personal tastes in cocktails.
18. Utilize a metal bucket to ice down beer, bottled sodas, water and wine.
19. If you are limited on space create a mini bar by placing all of your bar ingredients on a tray and set the tray on a sideboard for self-service.
20. To give added space to your bar elevate glasses or bottles of alcohol.
21. Place champagne glasses on silver trays and stack on top one another for a cascading effect.
22. For the champagne station stack glasses the same way as above to create a cascading effect.
23. For your vodka bar arrange high ball glasses on trays. Put a lemon twist that has been cut and tied in each glass. Display bottles of vodka that have been stored in the freezer to chill them thoroughly. To chill the vodka cut the top off of a half-gallon plastic milk carton. Place a bottle of vodka into the carton and fill the carton with water. Place the carton in the freezer and let the water freeze partially. Remove the carton from the freezer. Arrange slices of fruit in the partially frozen water by pushing them down into the water. Return the carton and vodka bottle back to the freezer and let the water freeze completely.

To serve your vodka remove the carton from the freezer and run the carton under warm water just long enough to loosen the carton from the ice. Let the bottle of vodka sit briefly and then arrange the bottle on your bar. You can also use a tin can to create the same effect as above.

"Wine is life." Petronius, Roman writer

24. A nice alternative is slush punch. You can serve various flavors or one flavor as a refreshing way to beverage your guests. You can also add alcohol to this recipe if so desired.
25. Hire someone to set up an espresso machine and serve coffee drinks to your guests.

I am drinking the stars! Dom Perignon, on his first sip of bubbly champagne.

SLUSH PUNCH

7 c water
12 c sugar
4 tea bags
2 c water
1 can (12oz) frozen lemonade
1 can (12oz) frozen Orange juice
Ginger Ale or 7up
2 c Vodka,
Brandy
Gin or Whisky (optional)

Mix in a large sauce pan 7 cups water, 12 cups sugar and bring to a boil and set aside. Steep for 20 minutes 2 cups water and 4 tea bags and add to the above mixture and let cool. Pour this mixture into a large bowl. Add the can of frozen lemonade, can of orange juice and if using alcohol add 2 cups of alcohol of your choice to the mixture. Mix the ingredients together and cover tightly and place in the freezer. Stir periodically leaving the slush in the freezer until frozen and you are ready to serve the drink. When it is time to serve the slush punch pour the frozen mixture into a punch bowl and add just enough of the Ginger Ale or 7 Up into the slush punch to thin it out so that you can ladle the mix into glasses.

Grape vines cannot reproduce reliably from seed. To cultivate a particular grape variety, grafting (a plant version of cloning) is used.

26. Utilize a large metal wash bucket for icing down bottled beverages.
27. Use wedding cocktails stirrers that have flags imprinted with the initials of the bride and groom.
28. **TIP: Allow one bartender for fifty guests to expedite service through your bar.**
29. For your punch station, cloth and skirt a six-foot or crescent table. Place an elevation in the center of the table for your punch bowl to rest upon. Set rock glasses to the right of your punch bowl either directly onto the table or on a serving tray that has been elevated by a glass rack and covered with a tablecloth. Arrange bunches of grapes, whole apples and oranges around the base of the punch bowl. Use a bread and butter plate as an under liner for your ladle and fan cocktail napkins for a beautiful effect.

Wine lifts the spirit. Olive oil lifts the palette.

30. If you are pressed for space in your home but want to set up a bar utilize a piece of furniture such as a bakers rack to display your libations on.

CHOCOLATE MARTINI

half-shot Stoli Vanilla
half- shot Godiva Chocolate
splash cherry juice
cherry to garnish drink

Place ice in a shaker and add Stoli Vanilla, Godiva Chocolate, cherry juice and shake until the sides of the shaker become frosted. Strain the mixture with a Hawthorn strainer into a martini glass and garnish with a single cherry.

31. For a different way to set up a bar utilize a crescent table that has been elevated by standing the legs firmly on top of concrete blocks. You need the height to enable your bartender to comfortably mix drinks for your guests. For a back bar be sure to station a six-foot table behind the crescent table for glasses and Lexans of iced down beers and wine. Always display your bottles of liquor as well as bottles of beer and wine on the bar itself so that your guests have a view of your selections and for ease of service by your bartender. Be sure to cloth and skirt all of your tables for esthetical purposes.

32. Have the chef carve a bowl from an ice block to use as a means of icing down your bottles of champagne. After you place the bottles of champagne into the ice bowl be sure to cover the bottles with shaved ice. This is a great presentation for your champagne service.

33. A unique idea for bar service is to create a hanging bar.

34. A liquor luge is a cool way to serve chilled vodka at a party. The ice luge is merely an instrument designed to chill vodka as it makes its way through a tube (swizzle straw or column), with a funnel that has been inserted into a carved block of ice.

"The wine cup is the little silver well, where truth, if truth there be, doth dwell."
William Shakespeare

ACAPULCO COCKTAIL

1 ½ oz tequila 1 ½ oz Jamaica rum 3 oz pineapple juice 1 oz grapefruit or lime juice Cubes of fresh pineapple	Shake everything but the pineapple cubes with ice cubes to chill. Drain into a Collins glass filled with ice, garnish with the pineapple cubes.

---

35. Create an liquor luge designed to look like a martini glass for your vodka bar.

36. Create an liquor luge with the bride's and groom's initials for a vodka bar at a wedding reception.

37. Another neat idea for an liquor luge for your vodka bar is to cut a square center out of a block of ice creating a frame of ice. Make sure that the edges of the ice frame are smooth. Insert the swizzle straw into the top of the ice frame. You can set your martini glass in the center of the square of ice and when the vodka is poured into the funnel it will trickle down through the ice and chill on its way to your martini glass. After all vodka is best served chilled.

38. Carve a bar out of ice and light the bar with a colored light to show off your bar. This is a great idea for a winter theme. Have a design or initials carved into the ice bar.

39. Another way to showcase your bottles of champagne is to have the chef carve a Lexan out of ice and place your bottles in the Lexan for champagne service. Be sure to light the Lexan. Champagne is a special beverage for a celebration. You want to showcase it.

The lip of a red wine glass is sloped inward to capture
the aromas of the wine and deliver them to your nose.

40. Use a tiered acrylic stand designed to hold bottles to display your bottles of alcohol on your bar. This

is a good way to add more space to your bar and add status to your liquors.

41. **Synchronized champagne service is an elegant way to serve the bubbly at your event. When it is time to serve, have wait staff line up with bottles in hands, in the back hallway. Send them into the room via a specified route and have each server stop at a predetermined table. When each server reaches their predetermined table let them stand for a few seconds and then give them the cue to begin pouring the champagne.**

42. If you want to have a full-service bar at your party, but you are not familiar with bartending, place a book of cocktail recipes on your bar for your guests to reference their favorite cocktails.

43. For a stunning bar setup, use a six-foot table behind your bar to house glasses and iced down bottles of beer and wine. Stack a six-foot schoolroom table on top of the first one and use that table to display decorations by placing fiber optic flowers, other neon or bar memorabilia and plants on the table.

44. Have the chef create a slide design out of a block of ice for a luge for vodka.

45. Have a martini lounge for your event.

Pousse café (push the coffee).

46. Coffee drinks are fabulous as an after dinner accompaniment to dessert. On page 82 are some recipes that we utilized at the hotel when we set up a coffee bar. A coffee bar does not require the use of an espresso machine. Just brew fresh coffee and prepare some simple garnishes and display along with liquors. You can have an attendant create signature drinks for your guests as they watch.

47. For a wedding reception decorate your dessert coffee station with rose petals.

48. Offer biscotti and cookies to go with dessert coffee drinks.

DESSERT BLEND COFFEE	
1/3 Jamocha Almond coffee beans 1/3 Espresso coffee beans 1/3 Dutch Chocolate coffee beans	Blend the three coffees by grinding in a blender. Use ½ of the normal amount of grounds when brewing your coffee. Store beans or ground coffee in an air tight con-

49. Create a menu to display on your dessert coffee station.

50. Place the initials of the bride and groom at the top of the menu.

51. For an ice luge on the bar at a wedding reception have the chef create a heart design out of ice. The center of the heart should be hollowed out with the bottom part of the center a flat surface where you can place a glass to be filled with liquor. The top of the heart is where the funnel and swizzle column should be inserted. The funnel and swizzle column is what the alcohol will be poured into so that it can travel through the ice and chill before it reaches the glass.

52. Let your guests make their own mimosas. Place pitchers of pureed fruits such as peaches, blueberries, strawberries and raspberries in bowls of ice and set them along side of champagne glasses and bottles of champagne. Guests can choose the fruit and pour a small amount in a champagne glass and top off with champagne.

COFFEE RECIPES

SAMPLE MENU

COFFEES

REGULAR_____DECAF

* AFTER DINNER CORDIALS *
KAHULA_____BAILEY"S

* ACCOUTREMENTS *
BISCOTTI_____COOKIES

Russian Coffee:
1 oz vodka
1 oz Kahlua
coffee

Scandinavian Coffee:
1 oz Amaretto
½ oz Tia Maria
¼ oz vodka
coffee

Spanish Coffee:
½ oz brandy
½ oz Kahlua
½ oz Triple sec
coffee

Irish Coffee:
½ oz Irish whisky
½ oz simple syrup
coffee

Italian Coffee:
½ oz Galliano
½ oz Kahlua
coffee

African Coffee:
½ oz Crème de Banana
½ oz vodka
½ oz Kahlua
coffee

Mexican Coffee:
½ oz tequila
½ oz Kahlua
coffee

Coffee San Jaun:
½ oz dark rum
½ oz Tia Maria
coffee

Top drinks with whipped cream and allow guests to choose their garnish. Garnishes include the following: whipped cream, chocolate shavings, cherries, orange slices, cinnamon sticks, sugar and rock sugar.

53. For a garnish place a lemon slice and flower such as a hibiscus to float in your drink.
54. Place your bar under an awning.
55. Set up a bar in your backyard staging it under a tree. Cover the tabletop with linen and place a decorative lace over the linen.

"It takes a lot of beer to make good wine." Lou Preston, Preston Vineyards

56. Set up a display table for bottles of wine to be served during dinner and light the table with candles.
57. Set up a cigar bar in a separate location at your reception.
58. Wine and cheese are great accompaniments; cheese brings out the flavors of the wine.
59. For an after dinner toast, serve champagne, in chocolate champagne cups.
60. Set up a slushy station. Have your bartender create frozen drinks as alcoholic libations for your guests to enjoy. Watermelon ice with vodka makes a refreshing slushy. Dry ice can be utilized to create an instant slushy. Place your alcohol and mixers in a container that is set in dry ice and create instant frozen goodness.

61. For your next bar hang signs behind the bar for a creative way to decorate your bar. Cut letters out of newspaper or colored papers and place the letters into glass frames. Words such as wine, beer and sodas are appropriate.

An oenophile is someone who loves wine.

62. At your next big social soiree have a reception before and after dinner. Serve cocktails at the reception prior to dinner and wine, beer and champagne following. Serve a red and white wine with dinner. Create a menu for your bars to announce the beverage arrangements.

63. Create a champagne bar carved out of ice for your next sparkling celebration. This is a great way to display your bottles of champagne as well as the accoutrements that go along with it. Champagne needs to be served chilled. It also goes well with a few other accompaniments such as strawberries, cranberries and rose petals. These compliment the flavors of the champagne. The ice bar becomes a way to keep the champagne chilled. The person that carves the ice for your champagne bar will use several blocks of ice. The bar will have to be assembled when all of its components arrive at the location site. The chef will carve square champagne chillers out of ice. He or she will also carve square bowls out of the ice to house the strawberries, dried cranberries and rose petals. The champagne bar sits nicely on top of a glass paneled bar. Of course the ice carving must rest in a plastic tray large enough to house it. The tray should have a place in which to attach a hose so that the water from the melting ice can flow into a bucket concealed by the glass paneled bar. Once assembled the champagne bar looks stunning and is a must for an elegant wedding reception. Remember to highlight the sculpture with colors of your choice.

Saludo! **means "greetings" in Spanish (a toast).**

SAMPLE BAR SIGN	A cosmopolitan is great as a signature drink at a party.
Enjoy Cocktails *6:30 - 7:30 PM* *Wine, Beer and Champagne* *6:30 - 12:30 PM* *This is a sign for a bar letting guests know what time cocktails are being served and what time wine, beer and champagne are served. The cocktails are not available all night.*	**COSMOPOLITAN** **Vodka 1oz** **Cointreau 1/2oz** **Cranberry juice splash** **Juice of lime 1oz** **Place ingredients in a shaker with ice and shake until the side of the shaker becomes frosted. Strain into a martini glass with a hawthorn strainer. Garnish with a lime piece.**

64. Create a small guitar out of ice, using a mold, to place in your drink glass. Dip the end of the guitar in melted chocolate and keep it in the freezer until you are ready to serve your beverage. Use a design that correlates with your theme.

65. For a unique way to display glasses on your bar, hang them above with wire.

66. **TIP: Ice water will chill your beverages faster since the ice water covers more surface area. Add salt as salt water has a lower freezing point than fresh water. Your beverages should chill in about 35 minutes.**

67. Use water to adhere the outside rim of your glass with salt to prevent it from falling into the glass.

68. Often times restaurants will offer a wine flight. A wine flight offers samples of various wines from around the world. These offerings are paired with various courses in a meal. Offer your guests a wine flight or a drink flight as a special way to serve alcoholic beverages to your guests. The drink flight might showcase various vodkas, rums or tequilas giving your guests a chance to sample more than one brand or type of a specific alcohol.

69. Display wine and rock glasses on a clothed and skirted six-foot table. Place one type of glass on one side of the table and the other type on the opposite side. Highlight the glasses with votive candles.

70. For a wine tasting place bowls of cinnamon sticks, chocolate, cherries and various fruits for comparison when tasting wines.

"In victory, you deserve champagne, in defeat, you need it." **Napoleon**

71. **TIP: Never freeze champagne; it effects the taste of the wine. You should serve champagne between 43 and 48 degrees. Do not leave it in the refrigerator for more than a couple of days.**

72. **TIP: Never forget guest safety. If you can afford to do so hire a driver for your event.**
If the sparkling wine comes from the Champagne region of France it can be called champagne, if not, it must be called sparkling wine. The monk Dom Perignon was responsible for creating champagne. We call this the Méthode Champenoise.

73. Create a champagne fusion bar for your guests to create their own mix of champagne and flavors. Have bottles of various flavors, edible flowers such as lavender and let your guests design their own drink. Be sure to display your bottles and fluted glasses on a bar that is lit from beneath.

74. Have the chef carve shot glasses out of ice to serve icy cold shots of vodka.

75. Give bottles of wine as a party favor. Have labels placed on the bottle that contain a photograph of the guest or guests of honor with information about the event such as a wedding. Be sure to send home the same wine that was served at the party.

76. For a creative way to display a recipe for your signature drink take a cork and lay it on its side and cut a deep slit down the length of it. Utilize a recipe card that has a photograph of the bride and groom and party information on one side and the recipe on the other. Place it in the slit and set it on top of your bar. Place a stack of recipe cards out for your guests to take home.

77. Use a large decorative container to hold bottles of wine, beer and sodas. Ice down for self-service.

78. At your next party serve Sofia Sparkling Champagne. This champagne comes in individual cans.

79. Winter is a great time to serve hot chocolate at your event. Utilize tiered acrylic stands to display Baileys or other liquors for your hot chocolate drinks.

80. You can purchase heart shaped sugars to use for coffee service at a wedding reception.

81. Have the chef create an liquor luge that has a spiral tube (swizzle straw or column), inserted into it. At the top of the ice luge will be a funnel that is connected to the tube and as the beverage is poured into the funnel the colored liquor can be seen swirling through the luge and into the glass.

82. Match your beverage with your color scheme by rimming the edge of your beverage glass with colored rimming sugar.

7: BUFFETS

Buffets are not a glamorous way to serve, but they are a more efficient way of serving food to a large gathering of people. I have put together a list of concepts to help you create a buffet that is functional as well as visually stunning. You can begin by choosing a menu, once you have determined what hot and cold foods will be served then you can visualize the layout you want for your buffet. Follow the list below and utilize the decorating ideas on the following pages to create a buffet with a stunning visual display.

When you decide on what food items you would like to serve on your buffet you can determine how much table space you will need for your buffet. Allow one foot of space for each item that will be placed on your buffet table. Remember to account for salad and dinner plates when determining the amount of tables you will need. The nice thing about a buffet is that you can serve simple appetizers or you can actually serve a full meal. I like buffets because they give your guests choices. You can serve meats as well as vegetarian options.

When designing your buffet be creative. Utilize six-foot tables as well as serpentine, crescents and half rounds to lend style and flow to your buffet line. Fabric choices are numerous. Use skirts or box your tablecloths for a tailored look. Be imaginative when searching for centerpieces or for decorating ideas.

Draw a diagram that represents your buffet tables. With a diagram in hand the staff responsible for setting your buffet tables will have an exact layout and will be able to set your tables quickly. Hotel Catering or an Event Planer has access to computer programs such as Cater Ease or Visio that will allow them to design buffet diagrams to your specifications.

Make sure that the buffet is set to accommodate the best flow of traffic. Try a two-sided buffet. The buffet should be set so that guests enter at one end and then exit towards the dining tables. If your room is over crowded with an abundance of dining tables set your buffet tables in the lobby area nearest your banquet hall. Place any action stations in a separate location to facilitate a quick flow of traffic through the buffet line. If possible have a separate station for desserts and a self-serve coffee station if it is to be available.

Be sure that your buffet is set up in the correct order. Salad plates first, salad items such as lettuce, tomatoes, carrots, onions, grated cheese, croutons and dressing in that order. Dinner plates are to be arranged after the salad course followed by chafing dishes containing meats, vegetables and starches in that order. Bread and finally silverware if not placed on the dinner tables goes last. If you are worried about cost place the meat items after the starch and vegetable items on your buffet. This allows your guests to fill their plates with less expensive items first leaving less room for the more expensive items.

Place dessert items at the end or create a separate station for your desserts. A separate dessert station will expedite the flow of guests through your buffet line. Place desserts on your buffet line after the buffet has been cleared of the main course or serve dessert to each table of guests for an alternative to a dessert buffet.

The equipment you will need for a buffet dinner will vary depending on what foods you are serving. Tables will be necessary for buffets and any actions stations, dessert and beverage stations. You will also have to set the appropriate number of dining tables and chairs to accommodate the number of guests that will be attending. You will need linen, napkins and skirts as well as plates, utensils, chaffing dishes, Sterno (fuel), silverware, glassware, coffee cups, saucers and elevations. Items such as burners, griddles, sauté pans and fire extinguishers will be needed if you have action stations set up in your banquet hall. Remember when you have your event at a banquet facility they will have access to any equipment that you will need. If you need special linen the catering staff will assist you in finding rental linen to match your color scheme. If you are having your event at a facility that does not have a full-time caterer available you can research companies that rent linen and other party rental supplies to find a company that is best suited.

There are many options for action stations. If you choose to have an action station or stations remember that you will need staff to man them. Some options for chef performance stations are: carving (steamship), baron of beef, Beef Wellington, salmon en croute, turkey, pasta, oriental stir fry, omelet, Bananas Foster and flaming coffee drinks just to name a few.

Elevation works well for adding space and height. Elevate platters of food. Alternate chaffing dishes elevating the second chafer the fourth chafer and so on. Also elevate decorations. Milk crates or glass racks covered with cloth make excellent elevations. Also utilize metal buffet stands to elevate platters to various heights.

Remember that a buffet requires less servers to man but you need staff to refill food and maintain the cleanliness. You also need staff to keep dining tables clean and refill guests beverages. One buffet line can accommodate 200 guests comfortably without slowing down the flow of traffic. The nice thing about a buffet is that it allows you room for any extra guests that might show up unexpectedly at your event. With a sit-down dinner the kitchen has to prepare extra entrees to accommodate any unexpected guests unless you order entrees to cover those guests in advance.

Sterno never rests directly on clean table linen as it may leave a black ring on the cloth. Be sure to set Sterno on a napkin or plate or place it directly under your chafing dish where it is designed to go. Never place lit Sterno directly on a table as it will burn your cloth. Also remember, never blow out Sterno. This is very dangerous. Use the lid of the Sterno to cap it off and put out the fire.

Next time you plan your event talk with the caterer and find out what they can do to create a spectacular buffet. Depending on the type of food being served it could be a less expensive option verses a plated dinner. Remember to keep options to a minimum as this will drive the cost as well. Be sure to have plenty of food available and utilize a small buffet to create a sense of fullness as well as visual feast for the eyes.

DESIGNS

There are many designs for buffets. Remember to consider the size of your room, its layout, the number of guests, the number of food stations needed and the foods you will be serving. If your room is small and space is limited, place your buffet in an area outside of your room. A hallway leading to your room or a lobby area outside of your room works well. If your banquet room is small, but you have enough space for it, place a two tiered buffet on a wall. Be creative with the space you have.

Utilizing serpentine tables, 60-inch round tables, cocktail tables, six-foot tables, school room tables, half round tables and quarter round tables enables you to create many different designs. Place a cocktail table at the end of your buffet to hold plants or other decorations. Use half round tables or quarter round tables as extensions to add extra space to your buffet or action station. If you have a number of food stations you might choose to use different table configurations for each one depending on its location and amount of space in your banquet room. Some buffets can be set up as double sided to better accommodate the flow of traffic expediting guests through the line in a more timely fashion. Cocktail tables may be placed in the center of your buffet line to hold decorations such as plants, figurines or seafood display. Some of the illustrations show the placement of plates, cold food items and chaffing dishes. Be creative, your buffet can become the focal point of your room.

You want to make your party different than others. Wow your guests with your creativity and taste. Buffets can lend themselves to such an opportunity by allowing you to showcase your creative side with decorations as well as a tasteful menu. Create a themed buffet to go along with the theme of your party or an eclectic menu that offers a variety of meat and side dishes to fill your guests hunger for food. Be sure to add action stations to go along with your buffet. Use the following ideas as a guide. Take these ideas along with you when you talk to caterers to give then an understanding of what you want your buffet to be.

THEMED BUFFETS

ITALIAN BUFFET
Salads:
Caesar Salad
Antipasto
Buffalo Mozzarella and Vine Ripe Tomatoes
Entrées:
Veal Piccata
Chicken Milano Style
Eggplant Parmigiana with Angel Hair Pasta
Vegetables:
Stuffed Artichokes
Roasted Vegetables
Breads:
Garlic Bread Sticks
Desserts:
Cannoli
Tiramisu

MEXICAN BUFFET
Starters:
Guacamole
Salsa
Queso Fundido
Tortilla Chips
Entrees:
Beef Tamales
Chimichanga with Chicken
Chiles Rellenos

Accompaniments:
Refried Beans
Rice
Shredded Lettuce
Pico de Gallo
Sour Cream
Desserts:
Sopaipilla
Tres Leche

COUNTRY BUFFET
Salads:
Coleslaw
Potato Salad
Entrees:
Fried Chicken
Pulled Pork Barbecue with Sesame Seed Buns
Fried Catfish with Tartar Sauce
Vegetables:
Mashed Potatoes
Baked Beans
Green Beans seasoned with Ham
Corn on the Cob
Breads:
Hush Puppies
Biscuits
Desserts:
Bread Pudding
Peach Cobbler
Lemon Pie
Fudge Pie

ACTION STATIONS

Action stations could accompany a buffet. For example a Mexican buffet could also have a Fajita station or an Italian buffet could have a Pasta station. You might have a baron of beef carved at an action station as part of your country buffet. As stated earlier, the action station is set apart from the buffet, which expedites the flow of traffic.

Action stations can be a great way of serving a meal during an exhibit where guests are expected to walk the room and gather information from vendors who have setup their exhibits to showcase the products that their company has to offer.

Your event might be a reception that includes action stations only. The list below gives ideas for action stations. Use this as a guide when planning your next party.

CHINESE STIR FRY
Stir Fry Shrimp or Chicken
Szechuan Vegetables
Sticky Rice, Egg Rolls
Have a cook stir fry ingredients and serve over rice in a Chinese to-go box. Use to-go boxes and chopsticks as part of your display. Place glass blocks in front of your burner to prevent splattering of food onto guests' clothing. Also place a bowl of fortune cookies on your station for guests to take away.

ITALIAN PASTA BAR
Linguine
Cheese Tortellini
Alfredo Sauce
Marinara Sauce
Shrimp
chicken
Onions
Red and Green Bell Peppers
Artichoke Hearts
Pesto
Pine Nuts
Parmesan Cheese
Garlic Bread Sticks
Have an attendant man the station to sauté the accompaniments and serve choices of sauce and pasta.

FAJITA BAR
Marinated Beef and Chicken
Onions
Red and Green Peppers
Flour Tortillas
Salsa
Guacamole
Queso Fresco
Shredded Lettuce
Sour Cream
Refried Beans and Rice in chafing dishes.

Allow the cook to sauté the meat and vegetables to order serving them over the flour tortilla. Guests can add accompaniments as desired.

CARVING STATIONS

Baron of Beef, Turkey, Ham
or Salmon en Croute

Set up a station or stations complete with carving lamps and cook to carve your selections of meat. Serve the appropriate bread and sauces to accompany each meat.

(Continued next page)

CARVING STATIONS, continued

Baron of Beef
Au Jus (served in its own juices)
Parker House Rolls

Turkey
Cranberry Relish
Orange Butter
Parker House Rolls

Ham
Mustard
Mayonnaise
Biscuits

BUFFETS: A List of 66 Ideas for Buffet Setup and Decoration

This list will provide you with many ideas for buffets. Remember to plan your menu first in order to determine how much table space your buffet will require. Be sure to include any props when calculating the amount of space necessary for your design. Enjoy my ideas and I hope they inspire you to create a fabulous buffet at your next event.

1. **TIP: Start your dinner by serving guests a plated salad course then have a buffet or action stations as a way to serve the main course. Serve a plated dessert or wedding cake that has been pre-placed for a wedding reception.**

2. A simple way to create an elegant buffet is to utilize potted plants such as ficus or ferns. Be sure to elevate some of the plants. Cover elevation and plastic pots with a cloth cover. If the pot that the plant rests in is decorative it is not necessary to cover it. For a potted plant that needs a pot transformation purchase decorative pots that you can sit the potted plant inside, hiding any unsightly plastic pots that the plant may reside in.

3. When arranging your potted plants on your buffet table be sure to set some of the plants at the starting point and some at the end.

4. For an elaborate buffet design, utilize a cocktail table at the beginning, end and center of your buffet line, to house your potted plants. Set up a cheese display on the center cocktail table of your buffet scheme in lieu of potted plants.

5. Utilize figurines such as chefs, chickens and pigs for a decorative element. You can purchase figurines from a restaurant equipment supply warehouse or Michaels Craft Stores.

6. TIP: Buffet food, hot or cold, should sit out no more than four hours for safety reasons.

7. For a wedding reception pin swags of pastel or white netting along the sides of your buffet tables. Use white skirts or box the tablecloths for a clean tailored look.
8. Purchase glass fruits and vegetables as props for decorating your buffet tables.
9. Use cake or plate stands to elevate various platters of food.
10. Display your food items on plates of different colors and designs.
11. Elevate ferns on plaster columns purchased from a craft or garden supply store.
12. It is important to use elevation on your buffet because it enables you to create extra space and adds depth and style to your buffet-scape.
13. If you are having a Chinese stir fry station or a buffet with a Chinese menu at your event utilize Chinese to-go boxes and chopsticks to provide a twist on the traditional china and silverware.
14. TIP: For each item that you place on your buffet table allow one foot of space. By using this measurement as a guide you will be able to determine how many tables you will need to adequately set up your buffet line.
15. TIP: Elevate every other chaffing dish. Place the first chaffing dish directly on the table and then elevate the second continuing to alternate in this manner until all of your chaffing dishes have been placed on the buffet.
16. Stack your salad and dinner plates in a pyramid design to create a special look on the table.
17. TIP: Restaurant supply warehouses have a variety of metal stands that you can purchase to elevate food platters on your buffet line. Remember to check with rental companies if you do not wish to purchase props.
18. Ask the chef to create a vase out of a block of ice for your buffet centerpiece. Arrange flowers in the vase and choose a colored pin spotlight to match your theme lighting the vase for a wow effect.
19. TIP: For a make shift buffet utilize a sawhorse and plywood to create your buffet table.
20. Cover your buffet tables in cloths that match your color scheme.
21. For a baby shower or other themed party, elevate food items on a buffet by covering cardboard boxes with a wrapping paper that matches your event theme.
22. Place rolled silverware in a decorative basket.
23. Decorate your buffet with bottles of olive oil, olives, fruit, vegetables and even colored water. Arrange glass votives around the bottles giving your bottles a shimmer.
24. Use decorative glass bottles of dried beans or colored pastas and arrange them on your buffet line for an easy way to decorate your buffet table.
25. Use a crudités or fruit display as the centerpiece for your buffet table.
26. For a wedding reception utilize a white tablecloth to fluff over the top of your buffet table.
27. Use a colored piece of fabric to fluff over the top of your buffet table.

28. TIP: Be sure to have the lighting crew illuminate your buffet or buffets to showcase all of the wonderful foods that are being served to your guests.

29. For a buffet dinner that a large number of children will be attending set up a separate buffet for them. Be sure that the buffet height is just high enough to accommodate the reaches of the children. Serve kid friendly foods.

30. For a perfect backdrop for your buffet utilize a window view placing your buffet in front of the window. A large window that showcases the ocean or a downtown skyline is a stunning backdrop.

31. **TIP: If you choose to situate your buffet on a sidewall allow yourself extra space for food items by creating a tiered buffet. You can achieve this by arranging a schoolroom table on top of a six-foot table.**

32. Utilize nature to decorate your buffet. Kale, cabbage, whole fruits and vegetables, berries and grapes make beautiful displays.

33. Leather leaf or ruscus greenery are naturals for decorating. Be sure to trim the stems before placing this greenery on your buffet table.

34. For a lavish affair utilize live mannequins to captivate your party goers as they walk through the buffet line. For a seafood buffet, center stage design, create an underwater theme complete with a mermaid sitting on a shell throne to entertain and enthrall your guests. For a country buffet create a stage in the center of your buffet and have a band there to perform for your guests as they walk through the buffet line.

35. For a wedding reception use rose petals strewn about the buffet table as a romantic way to decorate.

36. **TIP: Be creative when designing your buffets. Be sure to utilize serpentine, round, half rounds as well as six-foot tables to create an unusual flow and special look for each buffet line.**

37. Pillar candles are great as they lend a romantic air to your buffet table. Be sure to elevate your pillar candles at varying degrees.

38. Have the chef create a sculpture out of beef tallow to match your theme and reside as the focal point on your buffet or food platter.

39. **TIP: Candles are a great way to spotlight the food items on your buffet line. Remember for safety's sake keep all votive candles in a glass holder that does not allow the flame to extend above the height of the glass candle holder.**

40. **TIP: For another great buffet layout utilize two crescent tables and attach the ends of each table together to create a circular buffet. In the center opening lay a 60-inch round table to cover the opening created by the two crescent tables and use this platform as a space for potted plants. Be sure to cloth the center platform as well as the crescent tables.**

41. Ask your chef to carve a heart shaped vase out of ice as a centerpiece for your buffet table.

42. Make a fruit and cheese display the focal point in your banquet room by placing the station front and center. Upon entering the room guests can snack on various cheeses and fruits. Begin your display by placing a tallboy in the position you find to be suitable for its location in the room. Cover the table with floor length cloth and place elevations of various heights on the table. Be sure to place the taller elevations to the back of your display, creating a cascading effect. Display sliced fruits on plates of various sizes and set them on the elevation arranging the smallest plates at the top and largest at the bottom. Cheeses and crackers can be displayed on the table around the elevations and whole fruits

or greenery can be dispersed throughout the cheese display.

43. For a stunning dessert display utilize a croquembouche as your table centerpiece. The croquembouche is the French version of our traditional towered cakes (celebration cakes). Ask your chef or caterer to create individual croquembouche for each place setting.

44. Decorate a buffet that sits in front of a wall by elevating flower arrangements or ferns on pedestals placing them against the wall in back of your buffet.

45. On your dessert buffet, display various cookies that have been wrapped in cellophane and tied off with a ribbon for your guests to take home as they leave your reception. Also place a tag on your cellophane wrapper monogrammed with the event and date.

46. The dessert buffet is a great place to display various baked goodies wrapped in cellophane and labeled with the event and date for your guests to take as they depart your celebration.

47. To display silverware on a buffet line create an envelope fold with a cloth napkin. Tuck salad forks into the envelope fold with the handle of the salad fork exposed so that your guests can grab a fork as they exit the buffet line. Also create a flat tent fold to house knives, forks and spoons attractively.

48. For a salad fork display on your buffet place salad forks in a fan design at the end of your buffet line.

49. Have the chef create a buffet centerpiece by carving bowls out of a block of ice. Arrange fruits, steamed shrimp or other seafood in the bowls. Arrange cheeses around the base of the ice sculpture. Arrange lemons, parsley, bowls of cocktail sauce and cocktail forks around the display for the steamed shrimp.

50. For elevations for a buffet table utilize milk crates or glass racks that have been covered in fabric. Glass racks are perfect for elevating chaffing dishes.

51. Coordinate your buffet tables with your dining tables by covering both in the same cloth.

52. Make a dramatic statement by elevating floral arrangements or ferns on a buffet that is situated against a wall. Cover milk crates with cloth that coordinates with the colors on your buffet. Arrange the milk crates across the back of the buffet. Place floral arrangements or ferns on the crates.

53. If the party is a company event be sure to stage a menu with the company name and logo posted at the top.

54. Set up a candy station at your next event. Provide colored plastic Chinese to-go boxes with handles for the guest to fill and take home with them when they leave the reception at the end of the night.

55. For a buffet centerpiece utilize plaster columns as a means of elevating plants or other props to create a dynamic effect.

56. Fabrics that carry a theme are great for adding color and decoration to your buffet tables. Use them as overlays to a solid color tablecloth.

57. **TIP: If you do not have access to skirts for buffets or other tables that require full covering then box the tablecloths or use floor length linen to create a professional look.**

58. **TIP: Stage a menu in a frame and place it at the front of your buffet line for guests to read before they walk through the buffet line. Engrave the menu with the initials of the bride and groom, hearts or a company logo.**

59. Utilize lamé swags to decorate buffets. According to the Free Dictionary lamé is a brocaded fabric

woven with metallic threads, often of gold and silver.

60. **TIP: Cut the wedding cake before you open the buffet line. When guests have finished with their meal the wait staff can offer them cake so that they do not have to wait for everyone else to finish eating.**

61. **TIP: Any time you set up a station that requires burners place glass blocks in front of the burner as a way of hiding the burner. This will also keep the food when cooking from splattering all over the front of the table or your guests.**

62. **TIP: Be sure to place signs on stands next to each food item on your buffet so that your guests can correctly identify each item.**

63. Use a chalk board to pen your menu and place it on a stand in front of your buffet.

64. Have your chef create an ice carving to mimic your party theme. For an oriental theme use a pagoda.

65. For a Chinese stir fry station display Chinese to-go boxes in the front of the station with the chopsticks secured in the top of the boxes.

66. Sweet Dreams Candy Buffet.

Take a little treat, to make your night complete.

67. For a Mexican theme utilize sombreros, brightly colored fabrics, rugs in bright colors, piñatas, maracas, pottery and cacti as decorations for your buffet. Remember to consider your menu or the theme of your party and follow through with it.

BUFFET MENU FOR A WEDDING RECEPTION

SALAD:
Mixed Field Greens

Toppings: carrots, cucumbers, grape tomatoes, chopped eggs, cheddar cheese, sunflower seeds, garlic croutons, aged balsamic vinaigrette and buttermilk ranch

ENTRÉES:
Haricot Vert
Dauphine Potatoes
Beef Wellington
Chicken Kiev
Macadamia Encrusted Sea Bass
Garlic and Rosemary Rolls with Butter

DESSERTS:
White Chocolate Raspberry Wedding Cake
Red Devils Food Groom's Cake

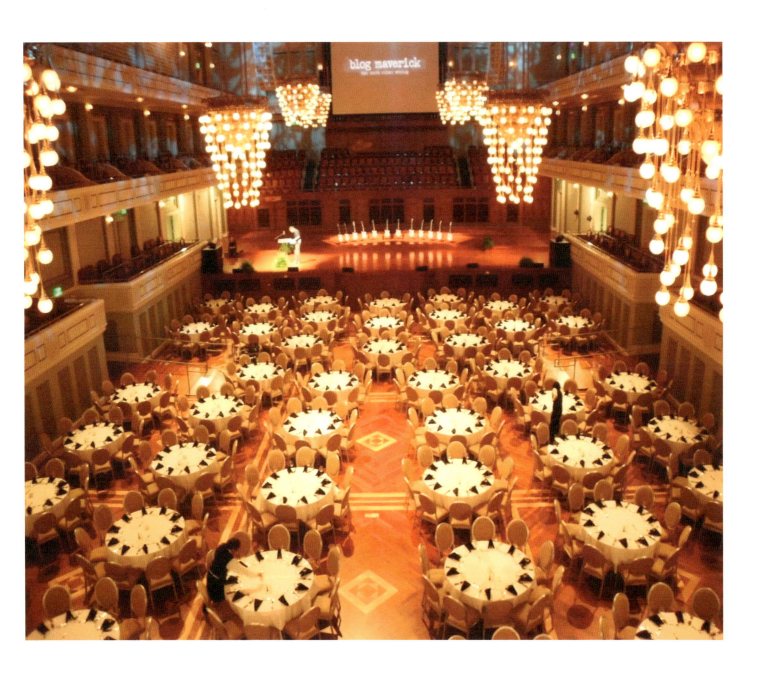

8: DIAGRAMS FOR FLOOR PLANS

How to Determine Your Room Setup

Everyone wants their party to be special. A memorable event that their guests will not soon forget. Not only will your choice of location, food, decoration and entertainment wow your guests so will the layout of the elements of your venue. Placement of dining tables, buffets and dance floor are important. Also important to a wedding reception is the position of the bride and groom, wedding party as well as the cake table in relation to where your dining tables reside. You want your guests to have full view of the bride and groom and it is also important to showcase the wedding party alongside of them. The cake table needs to be strategically placed as well. A guest of honor at any party can be placed in full view of your guests. There are many ways to design a stunning floor plan. It is simply a matter of how you arrange the furniture in your room.

Remember at a wedding all eyes are on the bride, but when your guests enter the reception site, you want all eyes on the wedding cake. Normally as guests arrive at the reception they enjoy a beverage and appetizers while the bride and groom and wedding party are busy taking pictures. This gives your guests the opportunity to view the wedding cake while they wait in anticipation for the newly married couple to arrive and be announced. Your cake is spectacular and no doubt cost you some money. You want your guests to be able to see it as soon as they enter the room. Some of the diagrams on pages 102 and 103 give examples for the cake placement in your reception hall.

Every venue is different, you must work with that space when determining the logistics for it. The site will dictate to an extent how your floor plan will look. Size and shape both play a role in furniture placement as well as entrance and exit doors, electrical outlets, kitchen location, restrooms, a stage and any other physical features of your reception hall. Also keep in mind the maximum number of people allowed by the fire department as fire safety is a priority. You have to work with the original elements in the venue space. When we speak of entrance and exit doors, for example, we refer to the fact that you must have enough room at those points so that guests can comfortably enter and exit your room. If you have a band you will have to place them near electrical outlets. If you are staging a podium and microphone they must have access to an electrical outlet. You want to ensure that your wait staff has a clear pathway to the kitchen in order to retrieve food for service. Every detail must be thought out carefully.

EVENTS YOU DESIGN

When we talk about the front of the room we are talking about the side opposite of the entrance. When you have a large gathering of people it is necessary to direct traffic. In other words you need to make every seat in your banquet room count so you direct traffic to fill in seats so that you do not have a lot of empty seats scattered throughout the room. When traffic is being directed always send the guests to the front of the room. When you direct the guest you never send them to the back of the room it has negative connotations. Sometimes it is difficult to direct guests to specific seats so you want to engage them in friendly banter along the way and make them feel good about the walk to the front of the room.

Your event space is a blank canvas. Transform it into a spectacular party space. Efficiently and attractively utilize floor space. Make use of the architectural features within the space. If a balcony is present, for example, stage the wedding cake there to create drama. Your floor design along with decorative elements represents your vision.

Guidelines to Consider When Setting a Room

1. When you enter a room your eye should go to the focal point which is the most important element of the room. The focal point might be a wedding cake, a head table, stage, podium or a buffet with an ice sculpture just to name a few. The room setup is based on the focal point. You need to know where the focal point of the room is so that you can properly set your chairs and tables. The head chair at a table will always face the focal point of the room even if the focal point is to be the entrance to the room. You also throw cloths on tables according to where your focal point rests in the room.

2. Draw a diagram that includes tables, chairs, buffets, action stations, dance floor stage or any other element that pertains to the room's setup. Use a scale of 1/16 inch = one foot or for a smaller space use 1/8 inch = one foot. Programs such as Visio or Cater Ease can help you create a perfect floor plan. If you have a caterer or hire an event planner he or she will be able to do this.

3. Determine the layout of your floor based on the type of event you have planned. Is it a buffet, sit-down dinner or stand-up reception? Do you have action stations scattered throughout your room? What about a dance floor? These are some of the things that will affect your floor layout. They help to shape the amount of space needed to comfortably house your event.

4. Remember that tables should be staggered to allow for more space in between each table allowing your guests more room to spread out their chairs. Every table in your venue should be spaced and lined properly. When determining the layout of your tables never obstruct the flow of traffic from the kitchen to the tables. When you design your floor plan be sure to allow room at the entrance for guests to enter comfortably. Always leave foot space around the circumference of the room for walking and space in between each row of tables as well.

5. Be sure to set your buffets near the guest entrance, off to the side of the room or in the center taking into consideration the flow of traffic and allowing space for guests to move freely around the buffet. Buffets require space in addition to the dining tables so keep this in mind when designing your floor plan. You may want to place buffets in the lobby if your banquet room does not allow enough space. Be sure that the flow of the buffet line leads the guest directly into the room as opposed to the opposite direction of the room.

6. For a reception prior to dinner set up any buffet tables, bars or cocktail tables and tallboy tables in the lobby area. If space permits you could set up your reception in the front of your banquet hall, but if it is stationed inside of your hall make sure that it is far enough away from the dinner tables so that staff can effectively set the tables. For a reception in a lobby be sure to move existing bars into the main room for dinner service. If you leave existing bars in the lobby your guests will have to travel further to retrieve a drink and unless you are on a budget and trying to cut down the traffic to the bar, you should have bars set up inside of your banquet room.

7. A dance floor will require additional space. Generally tables will be centered around the outside of the dance floor allowing for traffic flow around the dance floor. You might even have furniture such as sofas or cabaret style seating around the dance floor. Depending on the size and type of crowd present at your party you may or may not need a large amount of dance floor space.

EVENTS YOU DESIGN

SUGGESTED FLOOR PLANS

Event Floor Plan #2

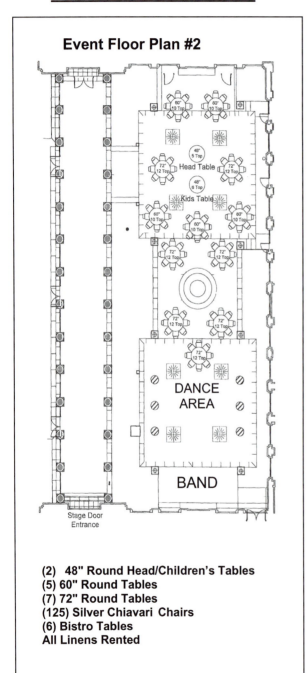

(2) 48" Round Head/Children's Tables
(5) 60" Round Tables
(7) 72" Round Tables
(125) Silver Chiavari Chairs
(6) Bistro Tables
All Linens Rented

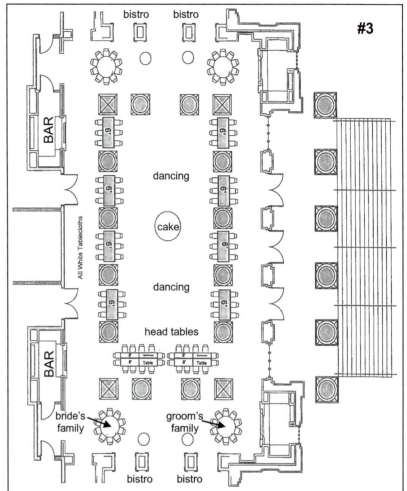

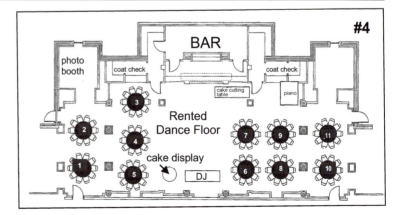

102

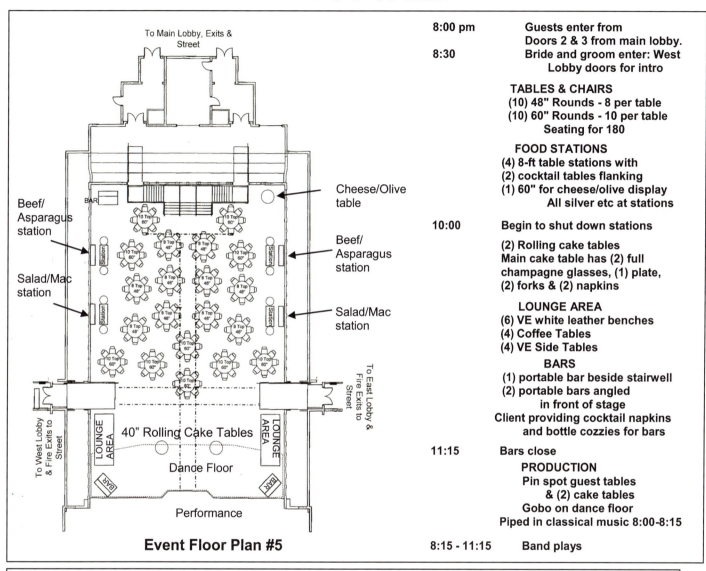

Event Floor Plan #5

8:00 pm	Guests enter from Doors 2 & 3 from main lobby.
8:30	Bride and groom enter: West Lobby doors for intro

TABLES & CHAIRS
(10) 48" Rounds - 8 per table
(10) 60" Rounds - 10 per table
Seating for 180

FOOD STATIONS
(4) 8-ft table stations with
(2) cocktail tables flanking
(1) 60" for cheese/olive display
All silver etc at stations

10:00	Begin to shut down stations

(2) Rolling cake tables
Main cake table has (2) full
champagne glasses, (1) plate,
(2) forks & (2) napkins

LOUNGE AREA
(6) VE white leather benches
(4) Coffee Tables
(4) VE Side Tables

BARS
(1) portable bar beside stairwell
(2) portable bars angled
in front of stage
Client providing cocktail napkins
and bottle cozzies for bars

11:15	Bars close

PRODUCTION
Pin spot guest tables
& (2) cake tables
Gobo on dance floor
Piped in classical music 8:00-8:15

8:15 - 11:15	Band plays

Page 102: Left: Floor plan with dining tables and chairs on one end of the space, dance area and band on the opposite end.
Right, top: Banquet layout with square and round dining tables lined around the perimeter of the room, cake table and dance floor in center of the diagram.
Right bottom: Floor plans for rented dance floor.

Classic Party Rentals
Delivery: 09/01
(10am-12 noon)
15' x 16' Dance Floor
Pick Up: 09/04 (by Noon)

TABLES
(2) 12-Top
(2) 11-Top
(1) 6-Top
(2) 9-Top
(4) 10-Top
Table #4 = Head Table
Captain's Choice
Napkin Fold

Page 103:

Large wedding reception and banquet.

9: FURNITURE

Furniture is an integral part of your event design. Most planners utilize 72-inch round tables, that seat 10 people comfortably, as a means for seating arrangements. Other options include square tables which lend more intimacy but seat less people and six-foot tables lined one next to the other to create one continuous banquet table which creates a homey feel allowing guests to wine and dine conversing freely with one another. Use table covers designed specifically for the table.

Be sure that the elements of your table settings all tie together. You have a myriad of options for chairs. Rental companies carry chairs of different designs as well as colors and even offer chair covers. You might choose a banquet chair and cover it with a satin chair cover or a cane back chair in which you weave a ribbon through the back of the chair. You might add tie backs in a color to match your color scheme and tie off the ribbon in a pretty bow around the back of your chairs. You might have enough space in your room for casual seating around the perimeter of your room. Set up a separate lounge housing a bar and sofas for your guests to sit in and relax while sipping on a cocktail. Furniture is another area where you can be creative and add a special touch to the design of your room. The list below will give you many ideas for furniture arrangement, ways to decorate with linen, lights and plants.

FURNITURE: A List of 84 Ideas for Furniture Placement, Table Lines, Chair Covers, Etc.
1. Scatter benches, covered with various fabrics and pillows in colors to match your color scheme, throughout your reception area as casual seating at your reception.
2. Utilize a large coffee table as a dining table at your next dinner party. Cover the table with decorative fabric and arrange pillar or tapered candles down the center. Arrange your silverware, china and glassware on the tabletop or wrap silverware in colorful napkins and place in a basket. Serve your meal family style if you have enough space to do so. Utilize decorative pillows as seating for your guests. Hang sheer fabric several feet around the perimeter of the table to create an intimate feel.
3. Have a decorator create large wooden boxes with an open top and a platform inside to set potted plants on. Think of this box as a large planter for potted plants. You will use these boxes to separate your dining tables and give a more intimate feel to the look of your room. Once the boxes have been placed throughout the room you will place benches, square dining tables and chairs around these boxes. You want to place benches directly against the sides of the boxes. Place the square tables in front of the benches and chairs will be placed around the remaining sides of the tables. Cloth tables and set accordingly. You could also paint the boxes in colors to match your color scheme.

4. For an outdoor reception utilize small cocktail tables with umbrellas attached to them to create shaded retreats for your guests to sit at while they dine.

5. Hang flowers on the backs of the bride's and groom's chairs.

6. Create a table of roses for the bride and groom to dine on in elegance. Utilize a cocktail table for the sweetheart table and cover it with a white floor-length tablecloth. Have a florist design the tabletop utilizing galvanized steel and Plexiglass to house a disk of roses that have been placed in oasis. Place the tabletop directly on top of the cocktail table so it will fit flush with the circumference of the cocktail table. The Plexiglass top will allow you to place silverware, glasses and china on the table.

7. **TIP: Living room furniture can add a relaxed feel to a banquet room full of tables. Arrange sofas fashionably decorated with throw pillows and end tables around the perimeter of your banquet room to create spaces for guests to relax and enjoy each other's conversation. Arrange flowers and candles on the end tables.**

8. **TIP: Set up a head table at a wedding reception or an event where guests such as dignitaries need to be in the forefront of the room. If a stage is available place the head table on it in the front of the room.**

9. **TIP: Create places for guests to sit and watch while dancing takes place at your event. Arrange benches with pillow tops and coffee tables around the perimeter of the dance floor. Arrange flowers and candles on the tabletops leaving space for guests to place their drinks.**

10. Utilize square coffee tables alongside benches for relaxed seating. Decorate the coffee tables by placing a square dish that is smaller on top allowing the guests room to set their drinks. Fill the square dish with glass pebbles or crushed glass and arrange pillar candles of various sizes on top of the pebbles or cut glass. Fill the square dish with water and place floating candles on the water. Light the candles just before your guests arrive.

11. Cover a 62-inch round table with a 85-inch x 85-inch tablecloth and place a round glass mirror the circumference of the table on top. Arrange silverware, china, glassware and condiments on the tabletop along with candles and flowers.

12. **TIP: For a small dinner party utilize a conference style table, giving a more intimate feel to your dinner and enough space to seat all guests at the same table. To decorate the space in the center of your conference table arrange flowers or potted plants in decorative containers.**

13. **TIP: Square tables are a perfect way to seat your guests at a dinner party lending an air of intimacy. Arrange the tables throughout the banquet room giving privacy to each table by placing tall vases, filled with flowering branches, spaced in between the square tables.**

14. A feasting (banquet) table is a festive way to serve dinner while bringing your guests closer together for great conversation and delicious food. Cover the table with a tablecloth in a pale color and lay a brightly colored table runner down the center of your table. Alternate short and tall flower arrangements and pillar candles down the length of the table runner to create a fun table design.

15. Create an interesting layout for your floor design by utilizing 6-foot tables for seating. Line the six-foot tables in even rows or space evenly in rows throughout the room to create a clean look. Cover the tables with cloths and overlays and line tall flower arrangements and candles down the center.

16. To create intimate spaces for a cocktail reception, line tallboy tables evenly spaced next to windows or a wall; place potted ficus trees and ferns in between each table.

17. When placing a chair tie on your chair be sure to tie off your bow so that it hangs off to the side.

18. For an outdoor reception by the pool utilize ottomans with differently colored cushions strategically placed around the pool. Also scatter highboy tables, cocktail tables and potted trees throughout.

19. For a wedding ceremony or dinner decorate chairs with long ribbons and flowers tied to the back.

20. Hang floral arrangements on the sides of your chairs to pretty them up for a wedding ceremony.

21. Arrange sofas and chairs that have been decorated with lavish pillows in front of a bar. Add coffee tables decorated with flowers and candles to the setting. This creates a space for your guests to relax and sip on a cocktail.

22. Instead of wood tables that require linen to cover them use glass tables for dining. Light the tables with pastel lights to add glamour to your room.

23. Use a long oval table for an elegant wedding party table.

24. If you use an oval table cover the table with a tablecloth and hang ribbons or swags of small flowers around the edge of the table.

25. Tie a bow with wide ribbon around the back of your chair and insert a long stem rose in the knot .

26. Pair a large Plexiglass block with a glass tabletop for a dinner table. Be sure to light the table with pastel lighting or candles. Lighting could be placed inside of the Plexiglass blocks. Contact an event decorating company to rent props for your event.

27. Cover your chairs with chair covers, secure the covers with three elastic bands of different colors.

28. Place a variety of stemware and plates on your tabletop utilizing different patterns and colors. Match your napkins to the table linen.

29. For a romantic table setting use a table that has a glass top and hang beads from the sides of the table. Arrange pillar candles on the glass tabletop.

30. For a way to turn plain chairs into beautiful romantic chairs tie netting or tulle around the backs of your chairs creating a bow. This will also add softness to an otherwise stiff chair.

31. Utilize a six-foot table or six-foot tables lined up next to each other to create a head table for a wedding party. The number of six-foot tables used will depend on the number of persons in the wedding party. Three people will sit comfortably at a six-foot table. Cover the table with linen and hang a swag of fabric entwined with tiny white lights across the front of your table. For a more polished look box the table linen so that the legs of the table will not be exposed.

32. To create extra seating at your reception utilize sofas, bistro tables and chairs to line the border of the dance floor. Arrange sofas, bistro tables and chairs in clusters at intervals around the perimeter of the dance floor. This will provide you with extra seating as well as tables for your guests to dine at while watching the other guests dance on the dance floor.

33. For an outdoor wedding ceremony, have your chairs set up in the round facing a stunning backdrop such as a lake or mountains. Chairs in the round lend a more intimate feel to a wedding ceremony.

34. If your event facility has a stage utilize the stage for seating unless you are going to use the stage for entertainment purposes. Place the sweetheart table for the bride and groom or the wedding party ta-

ble on the stage. Use the stage to seat guests if the space on the floor is not large enough to accommodate all of your tables.

35. Utilize a cocktail table for the sweetheart table at a wedding reception. Cover the table with a white tablecloth and pin a swag of greenery and flowers around the edge of the table. A small table will lend a more intimate feel.

36. To decorate seating at a wedding ceremony hang a white cornucopia filled with dried herbs such as lavender on the backs of each chair.

37. Use pastel colored cloths and a coordinated bow of fabric or ribbon to cover chairs for your wedding.

38. Utilize a variety of linen and napkins for your tables. Mix patterned tablecloths with a coordinating solid colored napkin or use a solid colored tablecloth and a napkin with a print or different colors on each side.

39. Cover tallboys with floor length tablecloths and then gather and tie the cloth just beneath the tabletop with a wide ribbon.

40. Utilize a taffeta table runner with sheer ribbons attached to the end that extends the length of the table to the floor.

41. Utilize tablecloths that are covered with glitter, spangles or sequins.

42. Utilize a solid color fabric such as pale pink on your dining tables. Cover your chairs with white chair covers. Tie a chair tie, in the same color as the tablecloth, in a bow around the back of each chair.

43. Utilize tulle or other sheer fabrics to cover your tallboy tables. Be sure to gather the fabric just below the bottom of the tabletop and tie with a wide ribbon.

44. Utilize lace as an overlay for your dining table.

45. Utilize colored news print to cover your dinner table.

46. For a sweetheart table cover a cocktail or square table with white table linen. Create swags out of sheer white tulle and pin the swags around the edges of the table. Cover your chairs with white chair covers and tie white tulle around the backs of the chairs in a bow. Highlight the table with a colored light of your choice.

47. Utilize a variety of boldly colored chair covers and napkins. Cover your tables with white linen and use flowers of vibrant colors in the centers of your tables.

48. For Mardi Gras use plenty of brightly colored lamé fabrics to cover tables and long shiny streamers to hang throughout the room.

49. Utilize lamé fabrics on your dining tables. Create swags with lamé fabric and pin the fabric to the edge of your tables to create a romantic look.

50. To create an elegant look cover your tabletop with a silk cloth and lay a mirror large enough to cover the table.

51. Utilize differently colored tablecloths on each of your dining tables to create a bold statement with your design.

52. For the bride and groom seating choose a wedding dress and a tuxedo chair cover. Linen rental companies should be able to supply these items.

53. To create a stunning dining table cover your table with a large round tablecloth, be sure that the cloth

extends a few feet beyond the floor. You want extra fabric so that you can pin the bottom edges of your tablecloth to the top edge of your dining table to create swags around the edge of your table.

54. Weave chair ties through cane back chairs leaving the extra fabric to hang down the chair sides.
55. For the bride and groom seating, hang a sign on the backs of each chair decoratively spelling out the words, "BRIDE and GROOM," Bob and Sue" or "Mr. and Mrs. Johnston."

56. Hang a picture of the bride and one of the groom on the back of each of their chairs.
57. Use an overlay with stripes in colors to match your table linen.
58. Tie tulle along with ribbon around the backs of your chairs.
59. Arrange 60-inch round tables around a swimming pool.
60. For a sweetheart table with style use a half round table covered in linen and decorated with garlands of flowers. Be sure to arrange the half round table so that the bride and groom become the focal point by placing the table in the front of the room with the bride and groom facing the guests.
61. For dining arrangements for the bride and groom, the parents and the wedding party, place a banquet table either at the front of your room or in the center of the room.
62. Line up sofas facing each other and place cocktail tables down the middle.
63. Use a square table for your sweetheart table.
64. Have a decorating crew set up large boxes that light up and hold posters. Use the boxes as the center in a cluster of square dining tables. Place posters of the bride and groom on these boxes or pic-

tures of the anniversary couple and family or a place that they visited on their anniversary vacation. Go with the theme of your event. Remember you are going to place benches against the sides of the boxes. Arranging tables and chairs for the remaining seats around all four sides of the boxes.

65. For the sweetheart table create a canopy over the table. Splash lighting in a pale color onto the sheer fabric of the canopy. Utilize chairs designed just for the bride and groom to give the feel of royalty.

66. Utilize banquettes along with tables that set against a wall. Place the banquette against the wall and chairs on the opposite side of the table.

67. Utilize lace table covers over a fabric tablecloth. The lace cover could have a floral design.

68. Create a canopy for the sweetheart table using sheer fabric. Hang flowers, crystals and candles from the frame of the canopy.

69. Utilize long tables for your dining arrangement. Create canopies to cover the tables using sheer fabric as the cover and decorate to embellish the design.

70. Set up a separate lounge area for guests to relax in and enjoy the party by using curtains of sheer fabric to section off the area. Tie back the curtains. Behind the curtained off area have sofas, chairs and a low lying table where guests can rest and place drinks. Be sure to arrange plenty of votive candles around walls and entrance to the lounge to create a special ambience.

71. Utilize organza sashes as tie backs to go along with your chair covers. Utilizes two different colors alternating them from one chair to the next.

72. Utilize elastic bands designed to fit on the backs of chairs.

73. Place a chair cover on your chair and arrange three bands of different colors on each chair back.

74. Place signs that have been strung together with ribbon across the front of the wedding party table. Use words such as "love" and "forever." Place the initials of the bride and groom on a sign as well.

75. Utilize banquet style seating.

76. Create comfortable seating at your next reception by using sofas and cocktail tables in groupings.

77. Create intimate seating for guests to utilize at your reception. Create a box with a flat top that will hold tall vases with flower arrangements. Arrange small vases with floating candles around the outside edge of the top of the box. Arrange sofas on all four sides of the box.

78. After you place chair covers and bands place a brooch on the bands to add sparkle.

79. Utilize curved banquettes and graceful padded chairs to create a 1930's Hollywood design.

80. Utilize clear or opaque acrylic glass blocks for end or coffee tables in furniture groupings. Be sure to light these boxes with colored lights that change colors.

81. Have your florist create "flower chandeliers" to illuminate your next gala. Create a box frame out of wood. String orchids and attach them to the box frame.

82. **TIP: Choose comfortable seating options.**

83. To create intimate spaces at your dinner hang sheer fabric from the ceiling in between dining tables.

10: FLOWERS

Flowers make great table decorations at any celebration. They can be used to decorate floor space or wedding altars. Fresh flowers are used to adorn wedding cakes too. They have a myriad of decorating uses. To save money choose flowers that are in season. Choose your favorite flower or flowers in colors to match your color scheme. Use greenery, fruit, pebbles and stones as part of your floral decoration. Be sure to have extra vases on hand in case of an accident and you need to replace a vase.

Contact florists eight months in advance and set up appointments to discuss flower arrangements for your next gala. Do not wait until the last moment to book a florist since they book quickly and you will be left without fabulous flowers if you don't. Be sure to inform the florist of your budget. If you have ideas for colors or types of flowers let the florist know at this time. They will be able to make appropriate selections to fit your budget. Be sure to take along a list of questions to ensure you receive enough information to make the right choice concerning the flowers as well as florist. The questions you ask will ensure that they are aligned with your vision.

SAMPLE QUESTIONS FOR THE FLORIST

1. **What information do you need to begin this process?**
2. **May I see photographs and real arrangements of your work?**
3. **Can you provide references that I might contact?**
4. **Are you going to be the florist who designs my arrangements?**
   If not can I meet the person who will be responsible?
5. **Will you deliver flowers to my event?**
6. **Will you place my arrangements in the proper settings once you arrive at the venue?**
7. **Does the price of the flower arrangement include the vase?**
8. **If my event is a wedding should I have a separate arrangement for the bridal toss?**
9. **Do you have vases, potted plants, arches or other props to rent?**
10. **If any substitutions should be required, such as the unavailability of a certain flower, how will this be handled?**
11. **Will this effect the existing prices?**
12. **Do you have insurance to cover any accidents?**

FLOWERS: 147 Ideas for Flowers to Help Your Party Bloom

The list below will give you ideas for stunning floral creations and a myriad of ways to use flowers in many different spaces. Copy any of the ideas you like and bring them along with you when you talk to your florist.

1. Have your florist design a cake table made of flowers to display your wedding cake upon.
2. Hang clusters of flowers from tree branches for a way to add a decorative element with flowers.
3. Display a small flower arrangement at each place setting. Let your guests take the flowers home with them at the end of the event.
4. Create a beautiful display by placing a round or square glass mirror in the center of your dining table. Sit a flower arrangement on the mirror and arrange candles around the flower arrangement.
5. Hang dry branches such as willow entwined with fresh flowers from the ceiling above a dining table.
6. **TIP: Be sure to supply vases, to hold the bridesmaids' flower arrangements, so they will be fresh when taking them home from the wedding reception.**
7. Have your florist create flower arrangements utilizing fresh flowers arranged in a round disc of oasis that has been covered with leaves gilded in gold.
8. Have your florist create arrangements that utilize topiary and fruit.
9. Have your florist create great displays combining fruits, foliage or flowers.
10. Utilize various elements in your flower arrangement such as Christmas ornaments.
11. For a stunning flower arrangement wrap gilded willow branches around a clear glass vase.

12. Use a tall, clear, glass cylinder vase for your flower arrangement. Arrange zinnias, orchids or other flowers in the bottom of the vase and fill with water to cover the flowers. Float candles on the water.
13. Use the same idea as above but place stones or pebbles in the bottom of the vase and insert the stems of the flower into the stones. Fill the vase with water and float candles on the top. Use smaller vases grouping three vases together on your table.
14. Fill a tall glass vase with cut orchids and cover flowers with water. Arrange candles around the vase.
15. To add elegance to your pool party float flower arrangements in your pool.
16. Potted plants such as hibiscus are a great way to decorate a party.
17. Fill the bottom of a clear glass vase with lemons, limes or both. Add water and flowers and voilà, a beautifully refreshing flower arrangement.
18. To create a tall centerpiece for your tabletops without impeding the view of your guests, utilize tall glass cylindrical pedestals and place your flower arrangement on top.
19. Use lights in conjunction with your flower arrangements.
20. For easy floral decorations utilize potted flowers. Decorate the pots to match your theme.
21. For a stunning entrance to your reception place tall columns on each side of the entrance to your reception hall and set a floral arrangement on top of each column.
22. For another stunning entrance to a reception hall place tall vases with floral arrangements at the entrance to your event.
23. Live potted plants such as ferns or ficus trees are great for backdrops for a head table or a stage and they can be lit with small lights.
24. Utilize a candelabra to create a stunning decoration. Adhere a vase of flowers with epoxy to the top of the candelabra. Adhere smaller vases to the arms of the candelabra and fill the small vases with water and place a floating candle into the water. Place the candelabra in the center of a glass box and fill the glass box with flowers.
25. Place pebbles in the bottom of a large cylindrical vase. Set a smaller cylindrical vase inside of the larger one. Fill the small vase with water and add three floating candles to the water. Place small bunches of flowers around the outside of the two vases.
26. For an eclectic centerpiece put a flower such as an amaryllis stem, bulb and roots still intact, into a vase filled with water.
27. For a beautiful spring centerpiece utilize fresh herbs arranged in baskets or clay pots.
28. Hang swags of greenery or flowers around the entrance way to your event.
29. Hang long flowering vines from the ceiling to create a beautiful decor for your event.
30. Arrange flowers in a circle or square of oasis that has been wrapped in a ribbon to match your color scheme. This is a simple yet elegant centerpiece for your dining table.
31. For a wedding ceremony backdrop utilize six-foot tall columns with flowers perched on the top of the columns to add grandeur.
32. Use vases of the same shape with various heights for your table centerpieces.
33. Have the chef carve a pedestal and vase out of ice carving the initials of the bride and groom on the side of the pedestal. Fill the vase with flowers. Be sure to have the arrangement lit with pin spotlight-

ing in either white or a color to match your color scheme.

34. Place a pillar candle inside of a large glass hurricane lamp. Arrange small vases of flowers around the glass hurricane lamp and add some votives to the arrangement.

35. Hang greenery or swags of flowers around windows and doors.

36. Set a pedestal in the center of your table and place a flower arrangement on top of the pedestal.

37. Tall glass cylindrical vases are great for arrangements of flowering branches. Arrange smaller vases of flowers and votive candles around the base.

38. The chairs that line the aisle way to the wedding altar will be the most visible so hang a flower arrangement on each of those chairs.

39. Place a flower arrangement in the center of your table and arrange tapered candles around it.

40. Create a ring out of oasis that will fit around a vase and cover the ring of oasis with fresh flowers. Fill the vase with flowers.

41. For an out-of-doors party situate your tables beneath trees. Hang wire from one tree to the next. Hang baskets of flowers from the wire.

42. Wire flowers in the center of a heart shaped candelabra.

43. Wrap vines of greenery around a column and place a flower arrangement on top of the column.

44. Hang extravagant floral arrangements above your dining tables.

45. Cover a tent column with fabric and hang tulips upside down from the ceiling around the column.

46. Hang tulips upside down from the ceiling of your tent.

47. **TIP: To create a sense of intimacy and elegance to your banquet room stagger standing pedestals in between dining tables. Place urns of flowers around or in front of the pedestal and another large flower arrangement on top of the pedestal.**

48. For another pretty centerpiece arrange glass bowls of flowers in the center of the table and arrange tiny vases of flowers around the glass bowls. Also dot the table with votive candles.

49. Utilize heart shaped mirrors in the center of your dining tables and place votives and flower arranged on the mirrors.

50. For a pretty table centerpiece utilize glass bowls of fruit and glass bowls of fresh cut flowers to arrange in the center of your table. Also dot the table with votive candles.

51. **TIP: Large spaces require large floral arrangements. A small arrangement would be lost in a large space but using it as part of a larger floral design would make it one component of the total design. Create a stunning display for a lobby reception by using large flower arrangements coupled with small vases of flowers and candles.**

52. Create a fabulous centerpiece for a large space utilizing flowers, a Plexiglass table, and candles.

    This idea makes a great decoration for an entrance way to your reception hall. The round Plexiglass table with four hollow Plexiglass legs is the base for your display. Here is a list of the other supplies you will need. Your florist can help you to procure these supplies and set up the display.

    1. One tall, round glass vase to sit in the middle of the Plexiglass table. Height is important.
    2. Clear glass vases in an assortment of heights. Square and round vases work well together.

3. Floating votive candles and glass votive candles.
4. Flowering branches to place in the tall vase and inside the hollow Plexiglass table legs.
5. An assorted of large and small flowers. Fill the four hollow Plexiglass legs with the flowering branches. Make sure the branches do not extend the height of the legs so that the tabletop will rest securely on top of the four legs. When you arrange the legs make sure they are evenly spaced and then rest the tabletop on top of them. This is your base. The next step is to place the tall vase that has been filled with flowering branches on top of the table. Arrange smaller vases of flowers and glass votive candles around the tall vase. Also fill some of the small vases with water and add floating candles and arrange them around the tall vase. Create designs at the base of your table by arranging some of the glass votives in designs at the base of the legs.
53. To offer the bride and groom an escape from the crowd during dinner at the wedding reception, set their dining table up in a separate room. To add a special touch hang a spray of flowers from the entrance of the room. A small room works best and can be decorated with candles and flowers for a romantic touch.
54. Utilize herbs in your flower arrangements. They smell great!
55. Utilize herbs as part of your wedding bouquet.

Juno offered orange blossoms to Jupiter on their wedding day.

56. Fill a vase with rose petals and then add an arrangement of roses to the vase.
57. Alternate bowls of whole citrus fruits with coordinating flower arrangements along your table.
58. Place round clusters of flowers in the center of your tallboy tables and arrange votives around them.
59. A deep clear glass tray or Plexiglass tray is perfect for arranging flowers and floating votives. Fill small vases with flowers and arrange them in the tray leaving space between each vase for your votives to float. Add water to the tray.
60. At your reception site hang sheer curtains against a wall where you would like to place a sofa for lounging. From the top of the sheer curtains hang groupings of freshly cut flowers and place a sofa in front of the curtains.
61. Wrap garlands of flowers around tall columns and place a flower arrangement on top of the column.
62. Hang wreaths of flowers on gates or fencing for an elegant look at your reception.
63. Swags of flowers, fabrics and greenery mix well to add sophistication to your decorating scheme.
64. For an elegant head table at a wedding party cloth and skirt your table or box your cloths. Hang swags of fabric or greenery and flowers across the front of the table. Scatter rose petals on the floor across the front of the table. Arrange trumpet vases, at intervals, in front of the table. Place pebbles or stones in the bottom of the vases and fill the vases with water and float candles on the top. Hang fabric to match your table covering on the wall in back of the head table.
65. Create a beautiful centerpiece for your table using large floral arrangements with dry branches included. Hang beads from the branches and arrange votives around the base of the vase.

66. For a backdrop for your wedding ceremony position columns behind the altar where the ceremony is to be performed. Place vases of flowers on top of the columns.
67. For a stunning visual backdrop use mixed materials such as flowers, bows, bells, birds and fruit along with lighting. Use your imagination. Make visually stunning backdrops for a wedding ceremony.
68. For a beautiful backdrop for your wedding place a glass cross or a cross made of flowers behind the altar where the ceremony is to be performed.
69. Hang willow branches that have been entwined with flowers and greenery and lights across the entire length of your tent ceiling.
70. Instead of chair covers, add elegance to your setting, hanging small wreaths or bunches of flowers to the backs of your chairs.
71. For an archway utilize greenery and small white lights to add elegance to your decor.
72. For a romantic backdrop utilize swags of two different colors such as light pink and dark pink. Entwine flowers and greenery into the swags and hang them behind the altar where the ceremony is to be performed.
73. Create a heart out of willow branches and flowers and adhere it to the top of your archway,
74. Create a dramatic backdrop for your wedding ceremony. Set up a small stage where your wedding ceremony will be performed. Set a round table on the back side of the stage. Cover the table with a cloth and skirt the table. Place a large flower arrangement on the table. Hang curtains on the walls on each side of the stage and tie them back. Place a potted flower on the floor in front of each curtain.
75. For a ceremony backdrop create a swag of willow branches entwined with pastel lights and hang the swag from the ceiling above the site for the wedding ceremony.
76. Use a metal archway and decorate with flowers and create stunning archways.
77. To create a beautiful backdrop for your head table place standing candle holders of various heights behind the head table. Set pillar candles of various heights on each candle holder. Place potted flowers around the pillar candles.
78. Utilize a fireplace as a backdrop for your wedding ceremony. Decorate the mantel with flowers and candles. Place candles in the opening of the fireplace and also arrange flowers around the bottom of the fireplace.
79. Hang a cornucopia of lavender on each chair that sits directly on the aisle way to the wedding ceremony.
80. Wrap ribbon that has been adorned with crystal hearts around a flower arrangement.
81. Monogram a fresh rose with the name of the bride and groom plus their wedding date. Place the rose inside of the napkin fold at each place setting.
82. Set up a floral arch at the ceremony site and place tall topiaries on each side of the arch. Line the aisle to the ceremony site with topiaries.
83. For a beautiful backdrop at your wedding ceremony create an archway out of willow branches entwined with flowers and anchor each end of the archway to a column for support and height. To attach the archway to the columns use potted flowers as anchors sitting the potted flowers on top of each column. Stick each end of the archway into one of the potted flowers.

84. Weave garlands of flowers or greenery through the stair banister.
85. Place sheer fabric over your tabletop. Add a colored overlay and create swags and hang flowers.
86. Wrap garlands of flowers around tiki torches for a backyard party.
87. Place a single flower to float in a small bowl. Add pebbles to the bottom of the bowl and floating votives too.
88. Utilize flowering tree branches with lights or lanterns hanging from the branches. Place the branches in a tall vase and use as a table centerpiece in a venue with large banquet rooms.
89. For a garden wedding ceremony create a trellis or use an existing one and hang flowers and lanterns from it.
90. Create a grid from wood or willow branches to be hung above the tabletop and intertwine flowers and lanterns.
91. **TIP: When decorating your event space work with your venue's architectural design. For example, place a garland of flowers above an archway or door.**
92. For a stunning table centerpiece place a low standing flower arrangement in the center of your table. Put a tall metal stand over the flower arrangement and place a mirror on top of the metal stand. Arrange candles on the mirror top. You could use bowls of fruit or bowls of floating candles in place of the flowers.
93. For a beautiful and unique centerpiece fill three short square glass vases with water and flowers. Stack one on top of the other. Arrange pillar candles around the vases. Use more than one stack of vases if you wish to do so.
94. Make a table by arranging flowers in a clear, large, tall glass floor vase. Place a round Plexiglass tabletop over the arrangement. Arrange glass votives on the tabletop.
95. For a decoration for the sweetheart table arrange the bridesmaids' flowers around the perimeter of the table.
96. Utilize a large potted flower arrangement for this beautiful display. Insert dry tree branches into the potted arrangement. Hang votives from the branches.
97. Attach a locket with a picture of the bride and groom on the wedding bouquet.
98. As a way to number your tables for assigned seating paint enough buckets, in a color to match your theme, so that you have one for each of your dining tables. Place a table number on each bucket and a flower arrangement in each bucket and set in the middle of each table.
99. For a decoration for the wedding altar place a square table on each side and set flower arrangements or potted flowers on each table.
100. Hang words such as: I DO, LOVE, FOREVER and YOU and ME above your flower arrangements utilizing decorative ribbon or secure them to a long skewer and place them into the flower arrangement. Create the words from cardboard and decorate with glitter or use fabric or paper with patterns on it. Use two types of paper, one in a solid color and the other with a pattern.
101. Use clear vases for your flower arrangements and fill with colored water.
102. Use floats designed to hold flowers in a swimming pool.
103. For beautiful centerpieces combine cranberries and lemon slices on the inside of your vases.

104. Utilize a plastic base that has a light inside of it and set a small fish bowl on top of the base. Fill the bottom of the fish bowl with rocks or pebbles, add flowers, fill with enough water to cover the flowers.

105. Mirrors make a room feel more spacious. Hang mirrors that have been framed in flowers throughout your event space.

106. Create spectacular flower designs by wiring them to tall metal posts that sit directly on your table-top. Secure a candle on top of the metal post.

TIP: If you have copious amounts of flowers at your next wedding reception or other event be sure to contact an organization that receives leftover flowers to give to hospitals and nursing homes. This is a wonderful way to recycle all of those beautiful flowers while bringing cheer to someone else.

107. Utilize clear rubber rings (aqua lights) designed to look like a diamond ring with a light inside. Place two or three of them, depending on the size of the vase, in the bottom. Add water and flowers and voilà!

108. For another cool floral arrangement attach the tops of orchids to silver or colored metal wire twisted into a spiral design. Be sure your vase is made of clear glass. Place some of the clear rubber rings (aqua lights) that twinkle in the bottom of the vase. Arrange the orchids in the vase anchoring the wires into the rubber rings. Fill with water. Place one or two arrangements on each table.

109. Attach a locket with a picture of the bride and groom to the wedding bouquet.

110. Utilize beaded garland around candle holders and as part of flower arrangements.

111. Utilize a cornucopia of dry or fresh flower petals to throw at the bride and groom as they exit the wedding reception and head off to the honeymoon.

112. Shower rose petals onto the dance floor as the bride and groom make their appearance at the wedding reception.

113. Have your florist create floral designs that make use of a single type of flower. Use a different flower for each table centerpiece.

114. Hang many strands of crystals above your tabletops to add glamour to your room.

115. Create an indoor fountain at your event. Float flowers on the water.

116. Hang bouquets and crystals from the ceiling.

117. Have your florist create an archway out of willow branches hanging assorted fruits and flowers from the branches.

118. Hang mirrors outlined with fresh cut flowers in various locations throughout your venue.

119. For a unique centerpiece cover small boxes with paper to match your theme. Place a small flower arrangement in each box and set them in the center of your dining tables. Arrange votives around the centerpiece.

120. Cover your square dining tables with a solid color cloth. Pin a printed organza sash around the top edge of the table creating a swagged effect. Attach a small flower at each corner of the table. Use this idea for a cake table as well.

121. Have your florist create umbrellas out of flowers for your bridesmaids to carry down the aisle.

122. Have your florist design a tree out of fabric and flowers. Utilize the fabric for the tree trunk and sus-

pend flowers above that have been entwined in willow branches.

123. Have your florist create a ring of flowers to suspend from the ceiling.

124. Have your florist create the initials of the bride and groom out of flowers and hang them on the backs of their chairs.

125. Create the initials of the bride and groom using sequins, rhinestones or beads and hang them on the back of the bride's and groom's chairs. Also hang a cluster of flowers.

126. Hang clusters of flowers and lights in trees.

127. Have your florist design the initials of the bride and groom out of flowers. Hang them on the door to the chapel.

128. Hang garlands of flowers above tabletops.

129. Have your florist design wreaths to hang on the doors to the chapel.

130. For a romantic ceremony, stage the wedding vows under a tree. Hang clusters and garlands of flowers along with lights from the tree branches.

131. Set up six-foot tables side by side to create a long dinner table. Cloth and arrange place settings down the length of one side of the table. On the opposite side arrange square vases of flowers and square glass votives.

132. Place an extremely large bowl with short sides in the center of your table. Place a tall cylindrical vase in the center of the bowl. Put rose petals in the vase along with your flower arrangement. Fill the bowl with water and float many candles.

133. Cover the frame of your mirror with greenery.

134. To decorate a room with chandeliers hang them at intervals across the ceiling. Drape swags of fabric from one chandelier to the next. Hang branches and twinkling lights from the chandeliers. You might also use flowers.

135. Use tall columns as part of your backdrop. Line the columns at intervals and drape swags of fabric from one to the next. Wrap coordinating fabric around each column. Place potted or fresh cut flowers in front of each column.

136. String roses or other flowers and hang them from the ceiling in front of curtains and behind the altar.

137. Slice fruits such as oranges, lemons or limes and arrange them on the inside of your vase before placing your flower arrangements.

138. Utilize colored broken glass as part of your floral arrangements. You can string larger pieces of broken glass to hang from your arrangement or place small pieces in the bottom of your clear glass vases to add brilliance to your display.

139. Strew rose petals down the length of your table creating heart designs out of the petals.

140. Set up banquet tables for your next feast. Line up glass mirrors down the length of the center of the table. Sprinkle the tops of the mirrors with shiny confetti or crystals to add sparkle. Alternate hurricane lamps, small votives and small flower arrangements if you wish.

141. For beautiful centerpieces combine cranberries and lemon slices on the inside of your vases.

142. TIP: Consider the environment by using live plants that can be replanted.

143. Have your florist place sparklers in your flower arrangements and set them off as the bride and

groom enter the reception site.

144. Have your florist create a canopy of flowers to hang above the dance floor. Utilize branches, flowers and candles to create a stunning canopy. Mirror your table flowers to reflect this canopy.

145. Hang a swag of flowers entwined in willow branches over dining tables. Attach small white lights.

146. If you are having your ceremony and reception in the same room utilize a long floral canopy for the ceremony aisle and when the ceremony is over send guests into the lobby for drinks and appetizers while the room is being turned. Arrange dining tables under the canopy.

147. TIP: Be sure to choose flowers that are in season because they will be less expensive.

INFORMATION TO BE INCLUDED ON A CONTRACT PROVIDED BY A FLORIST

1. The company name, address and phone number.
2. The date and day of the event.
3. The start time of the event and expected delivery time.
4. The name of the location site.
5. The address and phone number of the site.
6. The name of the on site contact person.
7. Deposits made.
8. Balance due.
9. What the cancellation policy is.
10. What items have been ordered along with sizes and amounts and the type of flowers specified.
11. If there are any special requests be sure to include them on your contract.
12. Any special provisions provided by the florist.
13. Signed and dated by the client and florist.

11: **LIGHTING**

Take your candle; go light your world.

Lighting Basics and the Professional

Lighting is another important aspect and yet it is the most overlooked element. It is essential to setting a mood. You want to wash the room with light so that guests can see one another. Guests look better and food as well when a room is properly lit. Remember at an out-of-doors event it is especially important to have enough light for your guests to see their way around. Use plenty of candles to create ambience. I think it is important to display many candles at a wedding in particular because it lends a romantic feel to the event. Candles lend an air of romance and intrigue to a social soiree. Hotels have audio visual staff on hand to help you with lighting. For a venue other than a hotel consult with an independent company. A lighting professional can help you create the look that is right for your event. It is easy to transform a blah party space into an awesome space with proper lighting.

Lighting is used to highlight important elements in a setting. You want to highlight table centerpieces with pin spotlighting to bring them to life. Place the spotlight on the dance floor to add drama. You should highlight ice sculptures to make them pop. To create drama in plain spaces where there is no color dress up the location by splashing color onto walls and ceilings or floors with lighting. Bring attention to a focal point by highlighting it to diminish what you do not want seen. Project the initials of the bride and groom onto a wall or dance floor as a unique way of keeping the focus of the party on them. Utilize lighting to showcase the sweetheart table or wedding party table. Highlight the band on stage for emphasis or create drama by projecting colored lights onto your plants. Candles also become part of the lighting experience and cast a soft glow into your banquet room. Hang twinkling lights above tabletops to create a starry night. Choose the right time of day for your event in order to take advantage of natural lighting. Remember it is also important to properly light the outside of your venue as well. This creates a dramatic first impression as well as lending light to guide your guests safely in and out of your event space.

Here are a few more tips to help you with your creative lighting.
1. Talk to the professionals when determining your lighting needs as they can help you to create the dramatic look that you want.
2. Remember proper lighting is also essential to the photographer.
3. Always remember safety when open flames are present by keeping a fire extinguisher on hand.
4. Research event lighting on the internet to be more informed when you talk to lighting specialist about your needs.

The list below will give you many ideas for lighting your event. When you talk to a specialist be sure to take a list of questions with you and as always ask the right questions. You want to ensure their vision is aligned with yours.

SAMPLE QUESTIONS FOR THE AUDIO VISUAL SPECIALIST

1. What information do you need when determining a clients lighting needs?
2. How are your services priced?
3. Will someone be on site during my event in case of problems?
4. How much time is required for setup and breakdown of the lighting equipment?

Be sure to ask questions in order to ensure your lighting needs are met.
Also be sure to get everything in writing.

INFORMATION TO BE INCLUDED ON A CONTRACT PROVIDED BY AN AUDIO VISUAL SPECIALIST

1. The company name, address and phone number.
2. The name of the event site.
3. The address and phone number of the event site.
4. The type of event.
5. The day and date of the event.
6. The setup and breakdown times.
7. Services to be rendered.
8. Any special arrangements.
9. On site audio visual specialist.
10. Any extra charges such as overtime fees.

LIGHTING: 136 Ideas for Creatively Lighting Your Event

1. For a beautiful way to light your dining table utilize a candelabra that has been decorated with gold branches, strands of flowers, beads or crystals.
2. For a centerpiece for your table utilize candle holders of various sizes and designs.
3. To add soft lighting to your bathroom utilize scented floating candles set adrift in a glass bowl.
4. Cover clear glass votives with pastel tissue paper or colored gels.
5. Utilize ficus trees wrapped in small white lights to set your room aglow.
6. Elevate glass votive candles by using rock or wine glasses that have been inverted and covered with a cloth napkin.
7. String Japanese lanterns with wire and hang them across the ceiling of your room or tent to create radiance. Use lanterns in colors to match your color scheme.
8. For an outdoors party string the lanterns throughout trees above your reception area. Use lanterns of various sizes and colors.
9. Create a stunning effect on your head table by alternating standing candelabras and flower arrangements on the tabletop. Make sure that you do not obstruct the view by placing candelabras or flowers that are too large in front of the occupants sitting at the table. Place small candelabras and flower arrangements on the ends of the table. Set up a schoolroom table in back of the head table and arrange large candelabras and flower arrangements on this table. In place of a schoolroom table use columns sitting them on the floor in back of the head table.
10. Fill a vase with lemons or a mix of citrus fruits as a candle holder and place tapered candles directly into the fruit as a secure way to stand the tapered candles. Use glass votive candles in place of tapered candles.

11. For a simple way to create ambience, line glass votives down the center of your table.
12. For a creative way to illuminate your cheese and fruit display make a candle holder out of a cantaloupe. Cut off the top and scoop out the seeds of the melon. Cut the bottom to make a flat surface. Cut a design into the sides of the rind making sure that you cut all the way through. Remove the cut pieces. Insert a candle inside of the hollowed out melon. Place the melon in the middle of your fruit and cheese display. For a fall design utilize small pumpkins to hold candles.
13. For a way to illuminate your food display at a wine tasting be sure to insert pillar candles into empty wine bottles and arrange them on your food table.
14. **TIP: Illuminate the walkway and steps to your front door on a darkened night by lining the sidewalk with votive candles and placing one on each step that leads to your front door.**
15. Chinese to-go boxes make an excellent format for creating holders for votive candles. Be sure to purchase to-go boxes with handles if you wish to hang them. Cut artistic designs, with an exacto knife, into the sides of the Chinese to-go boxes or use a hole punch to create your design. Place a glass votive in the center of the box. Craft stores have tools designed to punch out designs in paper products. Use Tacky Wax to secure your candle to the inside bottom of your to-go boxes. Purchase Tacky Wax at Michaels Craft stores.
16. Hang flowers and candles arranged in small glass containers such as mason jars from trees. Use flexible wire to create handles in which to hang them by wrapping the wire around the jars. String beads on the wire before attaching it to the jar. Alternate jars holding flowers or candles.
17. Wrap wire around the tops of glass votives for the same effect as above. Add sparkle to your votives stringing beads to the wire before wrapping it around the votive.
18. Fill your room with ambience by wrapping the bases of potted trees with small Christmas lights.
19. For outdoor ambience hang white lights from tree to tree creating a swaged effect.
20. Make luminaries: Place candles in brown, white or rice paper bags. Fill one-fourth full with sand.
21. If you are using tallboy tables at your reception, space them evenly across your reception area, leaving room to place a potted ficus tree in between each table. This creates intimate spaces for your guests to reside and mingle. Wrap the base of the tree or entwine tiny lights in the tree branches if electrical outlets rest beneath each tree. You do not want extension cords running the length of your floor space as this is dangerous and detracts from the overall look of your room. If trees are placed along side walls where outlets are available this will work.
22. Line the center of your table with votive candles and intertwine with dry branches, twigs, greenery or flowers.
23. For a wedding reception have lanterns hung from the ceiling so that they are in the formation of the wedding couples initials.
24. Cut tiny hearts out of tissue paper and adhere them to your glass votive candles for a romantic touch.
25. **TIP: When assessing lighting needs for your party consider lighting buffet tables and table centerpieces. It is important to highlight these elements of your party design.**
26. Hang a disco ball above your dance floor for a 70's feel at your party.
27. String lights around willow branches and hang them from your ceiling.

28. Hang large stars that light up from the ceiling of your tent, to cast a stellar glow upon your party.
29. To create a stained glass effect for your luminaries made from Chinese to-go boxes cover your designs with colored tissue paper from the inside of the box.
30. Create luminaries to light the aisle way to the altar. Cut heart designs, initials or special messages out of the sides of paper bags and cover them from the inside with colored tissue paper. Fill the bottoms of the bags with sand and place a candle inside each bag. Other designs include: wedding bells, hearts or doves. Use a stencil as your guide.
31. On a starry night, light the entrance way to the reception hall with luminaries.
32. Add personalization to an outdoors evening reception or ceremony by arranging votives in the form of the wedding couple's initials or last name on the lawn. Also use this idea for the front lawn of a reception hall.
33. For a stunning entrance way to your event create an archway utilizing willow branches entwined with sheer fabric, flowers, greenery and lights and hang above the entrance to your reception hall.
34. Suspend strings of white lights over the top of each dining table.
35. Spotlight an ice carving with white or colored lighting to create a show stopper on your buffet.
36. For an outdoor evening event hang pastel lanterns from tree branches.
37. Hang sheer swags of fabric entwined with white lights across the ceiling of your tent or reception hall to add ambience to your event.
38. Create a romantic mood in your reception area by spacing standing candle holders throughout the room. Place a pillar candle on top of the candle holder and wrap flowers, vines of greenery or willow branches around the candle and candle holder.
39. Utilize the same idea as above but instead of draping flowers around the candle holder pair the candle holder with a potted flower.
40. Strategically place colored lights so that they are aimed at the ceiling of your awning or tent.
41. For a romantic touch hang white lanterns that have red and pink hearts painted on them from the ceiling of your reception area. Also paint the initials of the bride and groom on the lanterns.
42. For a simple table illumination place branches in a tall glass vase that has been partially filled with glass pebbles and hang votives from the branches. Remember you need pebbles or rocks to give weight to the vase preventing it from toppling over when you hang the votives from the branches.
43. Wrap gauze fabric that has been entwined with white lights around a column and use the column as a stand for a flower arrangement or candle display.
44. Hang white lights and votives in glass containers from the ceiling of your reception area.
45. Attach wire from one tree to the next and hang glass votive candles. Situate a six-foot table beneath the lights for dining. This is a great way to illuminate the evening.
46. Purchase heart or rose shaped candles to float in decorative bowls of water in the center of your dining tables.
47. **TIP: It is not appropriate to use scented candles around food. The fragrance from the candles compete with the aroma of the food.**
48. For Valentines Day or a wedding reception partially fill tall cylindrical glass vases with heart shaped

candies and set a candle directly in the middle of the candies.

49. Utilize small lamps that house a candle and cover them with beaded lampshades. Purchase simple lampshades and decorate them yourself.
50. Secure white lights around the inside or outside perimeter of your tent top.
51. For a starry reception on a dark night utilize a clear tent and decorate the ceiling of the tent with thousands of tiny white lights dancing above for a twinkling effect.
52. For an outdoor reception on a darkened night create an illuminated reception area under trees by hanging strands of glass beads or crystals and votives from the tree branches. Arrange tallboy tables throughout the reception area.
53. Go Hollywood and have spotlights stationed at the entrance to your reception hall.
54. Utilize a profusion of lanterns in various sizes and colors and hang them at various levels directly above your dining table.
55. Utilize a Gobo to project the initials of the bride and groom onto a wall at the reception hall. According to Kinetic Lighting, a Gobo is a template that can be inserted into certain lighting fixtures to project an image.
56. Strategically place votives around a water fall, pond or stagger votives down the length of a stone fence. This is a great way to illuminate an outdoors reception on a dark night.
57. To float candles in a pool or on a pond arrange votive candles on a tray with sides and set a float on the water.
58. To create a beautiful way to light your reception area partially fill tall cylindrical vases with colored sand and secure candles into the sand.
59. Arrange pillar candles of various sizes on a decorative platter or plate and place the arrangement in the center of your table to create a luminous shine.
60. For an outdoor ceremony on a darkened night, light torches to add drama and romance.
61. Place torches at the entrance to your reception hall to add drama to your event.
62. Add light to your outdoor reception. Dot the edge of the swimming pool with glass votives.
63. For an outdoor reception on a dark night, be sure to place votive candles on your cocktail tables.
64. For your next backyard party hang lights across the roof line of your house.
65. Suspend willow branches enrobed with crystals and candles directly above your dining table.
66. For a romantic way to light your dining table set a lamp in the center of your table and place a flower arrangement on top.
67. Set your table design aglow by utilizing a glass cake stand to display pillar candles. Arrange pillar candles of various sizes on the stand along with smaller votives around the base.
68. For an intimate dinner table design suspend pendant lighting directly above and down the length of the center of your table.
69. For an outdoor reception on a dark night suspend strings of lights throughout your reception area.
70. For a unique way to light up your ceremony create an archway covered in lights to highlight the bride and groom.
71. For an outdoor reception hang lanterns from bamboo sticks throughout the gardens and reception

areas of your event.

72. Cast a warm glow on your surroundings by placing flower arrangements and candles in window sills.

73. For an illuminating idea for a reception lay rocks or glass pebbles onto a mirror and arrange candles on top.

74. Votives are a great way to illuminate your dining room table. Create a swirl design down the middle of your tabletop.

75. For an outdoor evening reception arrange tallboy tables underneath trees throughout your reception area. Utilize tablecloths with fabrics that shine to cover your tallboy tables. Hang lanterns from the tree branches directly above each tallboy table to cast a glow on the tablecloths.

76. Click lights are an affordable way to add light to a cake elevation and other food items on a buffet.

77. Create a stunning design at your next event. Light your dining tables from beneath. Set up a glass dining table and place a colored light underneath the table. Be sure that you secure any cords to the floor to prevent any accidents from occurring. Cover your table with a floor-length white tablecloth. Arrange your silverware, china and glassware on the tabletop. Place a flower arrangement in the center of the table. When it is time for guests to arrive turn on the light under your table. You will be amazed at how glamorous your table setting looks. At an event where you have more than one table use different colored lights at each table.

78. Utilize glass hurricane lamps to house your pillar candles and sit them in the center of your table for decoration. Place the pillar candle on top of a coordinating charger plate or a square mirror. Choose hurricane lamps that match your color scheme or have a specific design that matches your theme.

79. Have your audio visual technicians use Gobos to place the name or initials of the bride and groom onto the side of your tent.

80. Have your audio visual technicians light the dance floor with the bride's and groom's name or initials.

81. If your wedding ceremony is in a garden area that has iron railing, cover the iron railing with small white lights, to create a romantic backdrop for your ceremony setting.

82. For an outdoor reception position large and small candles throughout your reception area.

83. At your next event have your band spotlighted in a color such as red or one to match your color scheme. Do not highlight the lead singer instead use natural light to keep the lead singer front and center.

84. Be creative when lighting the band. Utilize a light color on the stage for the band and splash a darker color on the back wall of the stage. Your audio visual technician can suggest ways to light your event that will make your dining tables, buffets, ice carvings and other elements of your event pop.

85. Create a platform holding candles hung from the ceiling of a tent. Cut pieces of wood into squares and then cut designs into the wood. Attach chains to the corners of the wood so that it can be hung. Arrange pillar candles in between designs after hanging. Add a heart design cut out of wood.

86. Create designs on columns with various colored lights and Gobos. Splash the bride's and groom's initials on columns. Ask your lighting expert to help.

87. For your table centerpiece place either a square or round mirror in the center of your table. Place glass votives on the mirror and surround them with sparkles or confetti.

88. Attach picture frames together to make a screen. Remove the cardboard or paper that rests in the frame and discard. Adhere colored tissue paper to the glass plate of the frame with Tacky Wax. Secure the glass in place with the tabs on the sides of the picture frame so that the glass does not fall out. Place many screens around the perimeter of the room and backlight each one to create a colorful glow. Or replace tissue paper with photographs of the guest of honor.
89. Hang crystals from the bottoms of lanterns.
90. **TIP: Always think safety first. Be sure that the votives you place in your glass holders do not extend above the rim of the holder. You want the flame to be contained within the glass holder.**
91. At your next event set up lighting (Varilite) in your room that changes color every 30 minutes.
92. For a softening effect in a room, hang sheer fabrics along the walls, light the walls of fabric with colored lights.
93. Hang chandeliers from the ceiling of your tent. Hang flowers from the chandelier as well as greenery and strands of crystals.
94. Create a wall of twinkling lights as a backdrop for your wedding ceremony.
95. Attach tiny white or colored lights around your door and window frames for a twinkling effect.
96. Create a beautiful chandelier or chandeliers for your event. "Always be creative!" is my motto. Create a square box frame out of wire. Wrap it in sheer fabric in the color of your choice or paint it. This frame will be attached to the ceiling of your tent or venue. It will be the base of your chandelier. From this base you will hang strands of crystals or opaque spangles. The strands will hang from inside of the box. Be sure they are of varying lengths. The next step is to hang silver disco balls in between the strands of crystals. Utilize disco balls, depending on the size of your chandelier they will add sparkle and whimsy to your chandelier. Have your lighting crew place a stand light on each side of the room and aim them directly at the chandelier. Voilà, you have sparkle from a faux chandelier.
97. Use a slide projector to project the image of the bride and groom onto a wall at the reception site.
98. Purchase wrought iron centerpieces for your table and wrap them with grapevines; utilize hanging votive candles.
99. Cover the head table with sheer fabric and pin swags of tulle down the length of the table. Securely place lighting beneath the table ensuring that all cords have been taped to the floor and covered to prevent guests from tripping.
100. Create lanterns from wax paper bags and attach streamers, hearts or flowers from the bottom of them. String the lanterns and hang them from trees or ceilings.
101. Have your lighting specialist project red hearts on walls with Gobos.
102. **TIP: Be sure to pour a small amount of water into the bottoms of glass votives. This prevents the votive candle from sticking to the inside of the glass container.**
103. Have your decorator create a metal frame in which to encompass a sofa. Cover the frame with sheer fabric. Hang a chandelier from the center of the frame directly above the sofa. Backlight the sofa if you choose to do so. Also add embellishments to the sheer fabric.
104. Hang candles with shades directly above your dining tables.

105. Utilize square trays to arrange glass votives for your table centerpiece.
106. Have your florist create a square of greenery to hang from your ceiling. Attach a lantern, flowers and crystals as part of this arrangement.
107. Illuminate food on buffets by hanging lanterns directly above.
108. Use Gobos to project the initials of the bride and groom onto the wedding cake table. Project other images or messages such as, I LOVE YOU.
109. Project the initials of the bride and groom on to a white screen.
110. For an outdoors ceremony line your seating in rows beneath trees. Hang many brightly colored lanterns above your seating.
111. Create chandeliers to hang over your tabletops utilizing willow branches. Entwine tiny white lights into the branches. Use a large profusion of branches grouped and tied together. Hang them above your tabletops.
112. Carve your pumpkin or melon to hold a candle. Cut the top off of the fruit. Hollow out the interior and then carve a heart with the first letter of the bridal couple's last name.
113. Use a drill to make holes in a pumpkin that has been hollowed out. Place the pumpkin open end down over a candle.
114. Create a wire frame that extends around the circumference of your pool. Hang lanterns or lights and even flowers from the wire frame.
115. Place huge glass holders in the centers of your dining tables and float candles.
116. Utilize trumpet vases to float votive candles.
117. Use tall glasses as a receptacle to float candles for your display.
118. Decorate your votives by wrapping wire ribbon around them and tie the ribbon in a bow. Choose colors or patterns to match your style.
119. Place a wire ribbon around the top portion of a tall vase and coordinate wire ribbon around your votives. Place the vase in the center of your table and fill with water to float a flower. Arrange the votives around the base of your vase.
120. Decorate votives with beads of various sizes that have been strung on wire and wrapped around your glass votive.
121. Cover your walls in white fabric (curtains), lighting them in the appropriate colors.
122. Stand mirrors against walls to create beautiful reflections. Light them if you wish to do so.
123. Have a heart cut out of wood to hang from your ceiling. Arrange crystals and votives in the center of the frame and hang some of them from the edge of the frame.
124. To create unique lighting options for your party take square pieces of glass and paint designs on them to match your theme. Hang them against the wall and backlight them.
125. For a winter wonderland effect, use lighting to create a northern lights effect.
126. Use moving lights that change colors, shapes and patterns.
127. Rent illuminated cubes to utilize for tables at your next reception.
128. Decorate your votives by wrapping wire strung with beads around them and tie in a bow. Choose colors or patterns to compliment your style.

129. TIP: Remember to consider the size of your room when creating flower arrangements for your tables.

130. Purchase heart shaped trays and arrange candles on them for the center of your table.

131. Utilize customized artwork for a Gobo.

132. TIP: Remember to keep your party safe by lighting any dark areas at an outside event. It is important to keep walkways to your venue, entrances and exits of a building well lit.

133. If your reception is staged next to water such as a swimming pool be sure to light the water in a color that is part of your decorating scheme. Ask your lighting specialist about this.

134. To add color and opulence to your banquet setting, hang drapery in colors to match your color scheme around the walls of the banquet hall. Hang swags across the top of your drapery. Light your walls with white lighting.

135. Have your audio visual technician use Gobos to project the names of the bride and groom or a company logo onto the floor in front of your buffet.

136. If you have open space in the entrance to your banquet room, use Gobos to project the names of the bride and groom or a company logo onto the floor or a wall.

12: CHUPPAHS, ARCHES, GAZEBOS, TENTS AND BACKDROPS

This section showcases creative ideas for chuppahs, arches, gazebos, tents and backdrops. I have grouped the ideas for these items in the same section. Each category has been listed separately so that you can easily find what you are searching for. Utilize any of these ideas to turn your celebration into a show stopper.

CHUPPAHS, ARCHES, GAZEBOS, TENTS and BACKDROPS: 81 Ideas

CHUPPAHS

The chuppah is the structure that the bride and groom stands under while taking their wedding vows. It represents Gods' existence, sanctuary and care. The chuppah is a Jewish canopy and is part of a traditional Jewish wedding ceremony.

EVENTS YOU DESIGN

1. Create a box frame any size desired and attach it to four wooden posts that are high enough to walk under. Decorate the frame with sheer fabric and flowers or greenery.
2. Create a box or circular frame using willow branches. Anchor the frame to the ceiling or stand it upright using four wooden posts. For something a little more fancy decorate the chuppahs with flowers and greenery.
3. Create a frame from one of the ideas above. Utilize sheer gauze or netting to cover it. Adhere three flower arrangements or as many as desired to the top of the front of your frame.
4. **TIP: Chuppahs are easy to design. Basically all you need is three branches and masking tape to hold the three branches together. Adhere one branch to a second branch basically creating a 90 degree angle. Adhere the third branch to the other two branches to create a second 90 degree angle. Now all you need are two potted flowers of considerable size and some sheer fabric. Stand the frame upright by placing each of the two ends of the frame into each of the potted flowers. Decorate the frame by draping the sheer fabric around the frame.**
5. Create a stage for your ceremony placing it in the center of chairs that have been arranged theater style. Place your chuppahs on the stage and decorate it with sheer fabric and flowers.
6. Set up your chuppahs among the reception tables. Place your chuppahs in a prominent location in your reception hall. Be sure to have an aisle and line it with flowers and glass votive candles. Your dining tables will line the aisle too. Place sheer fabric behind the chuppahs and backlight it for the ceremony.
7. For another beautiful design for a chuppah have your florist create a ring of flowers and greenery. Hang them from the ceiling of your tent with rope that has been covered with ribbons in a color to match your color palette. Let the ribbons extend below the ring of flowers.
8. For a wedding ceremony set up a stage in a prominent location. Position your chuppahs on the stage and hang flowers from the chuppahs. Place on stage a large arrangement of fresh cut or potted flowers on a table in the background.
9. Hang leis of flowers on the chuppah.
10. Cover your chuppah with many strands of pastel ribbons.
11. For your chuppah use swags of flowers along with strands of flowers as a romantic way to decorate the ceremony site.
12. Be creative when designing a mandap (Indian canopy used for the wedding ceremony), for your wedding. Have your florist design one that is made from acrylic with hollow columns to hold hanging crystals. Create trays designed to connect the four columns at the top so that you can fill them with water and float flowers in them.
13. Create a chuppah with the box design as mentioned under idea number one. Cover the frame and wooden posts with decorative paper or paint a design on it.
14. Reuse your chuppah for a beautiful way to cover your wedding cake.
15. Utilize a mandap. Have your florist design one that is made from hollow acrylic columns. Also create acrylic trays that will connect the four columns at the top and float flowers in them. Hang flowers or crystals from the inside of the hollow columns.

ARCHES

An arch could represent a chuppah or simply frame the bride and groom during the repeating of the vows.

1. For a beautiful background for a wedding ceremony create an arch using willow branches. Wrap white lights around the branches and arrange flowers throughout. Place the ends in potted flowers to stand upright. The archway is perfect for the bride and groom to stand under for the wedding vows.
2. Create a stunning backdrop for your wedding ceremony by staging it in front of a large window with a nice view. Place your arch in front of the window and decorate it with ribbons, crystals and flowers.
3. **TIP: You can purchase a wire arch at Michaels Craft Stores and decorate it yourself or ask your florist to do so.**
4. **TIP: The arch could be used as the chuppahs are for a Jewish wedding ceremony.**
5. Ask your florist to decorate an archway with grape vines and bunches of grapes. You could use artificial fruit.
6. Hang flowers from your arch to create a romantic look.
7. Create an arch using tree branches that have been wired together.
8. Use multiple arches next to each other. Decorate them with flowers.
9. Create a triple arch and cover it with garlands of flowers.
10. Create an arch from willow branches and adhere it to the tops of two tall columns by placing the ends of the branches into the dirt of two potted flowers and sit each pot on top of one of the two columns. Arrange garlands of fresh flowers around the branches.
11. Create an arch out of branches and decorate it with flowers. Support the arch with tall columns and secure it to the columns as directed above. Create a heart out of willow branches or purchase one at a craft store to adorn the top of the arch. Decorate the heart with smaller flowers and join the heart to the top of the arch. This is a romantic way to showcase the bride and groom at their ceremony.
12. After you have designed your arch and decorated it with flowers be sure to hang glass votives from it.
13. Potpourri and greenery hanging from an arch makes a very romantic display.
14. Use willow branches to create an arch decorating it with apples, oranges, lemons, limes, clusters of grapes or artificial fruit.

GAZEBOS

A gazebo does not have religious significance to a wedding ceremony, but like the chuppah, is a canopy in which to stage the ceremony under.

1. Have your ceremony under a gazebo in a garden; decorate it with swags of sheer fabric and flowers for a romantic appearance.
2. To lend romance to a wedding ceremony create an arch at the entrance of your isle and decorate it with flowers. For the wedding ceremony utilize a gazebo. Place flowers on top of the gazebo. For the floor of the gazebo arrange potted ferns and flowers to fill in the empty spaces and add romance to the total look of the ceremony.

3. Bouquets and greenery hanging from a gazebo makes a very romantic display.
4. Flowers or vines trailing the columns of a gazebo make for a romantic showcase at a wedding.
5. Utilize an iron gazebo for the bride and groom to stand beneath. Decorate the gazebo by hanging crystals and candles from the center of the ceiling of the gazebo.
6. For a wedding ceremony set under a gazebo, decorate the gazebo with swags of sheer fabric, hang crystals and clear glass votive from the gazebo ceiling.
7. Hang small bunches of flowers and crystals from a gazebo.
8. Arrange tiny white lights on the roof top of your gazebo.
9. Decorate the columns of your gazebo with fabric and flowers.

TENTS

Tents of course can be used to house a party or stage a wedding ceremony as well as serve as a portable kitchen and rest rooms for an outdoor event. Tents can be air conditioned as well as heated. Emergency generators will be on hand to achieve this. Tents come in a variety of forms and sizes. There are Standard Frame, Pole Tents, High Peak, Canopy, Tension Tents and Clear Span Tents to choose from. You will find it prudent to contact a tent rental company and ask for advice on selecting a tent.

1. For an event inside of an auditorium have a tent large enough to house your event set up inside of the auditorium. Be sure to install carpet on the floor. This is a unique way to disguise concrete walls and floors.
2. Design a square or wooden canopy and cover it with sheer fabric. Place the bridal couple's table inside. Decorate the canopy with flowers. This is an alternative to staging the wedding couples dinner table in a separate room. You could also place a sofa underneath the canopy. The bride and groom can rest or have guests join them while having a more intimate conversation.
3. For an outdoor dinner, construct a frame out of wood to create an awning, hang sheer fabric from the wood frame to allow for a romantic feel. Utilize a chandelier that holds candles, to illuminate the tent, placing the chandelier in the center of your dining table.
4. For a wedding reception that is to be outside set up a small tent for the bride and groom to take their repast in. Hang a round floral ball from the entrance. Place a small table with flowers for dining.
5. Create frames out of wood to stand over your dining tables. Weave dry branches or flowers into them. Drape sheer fabric over them and hang votive candles. If the fabric is as close as eight inches to the candles it could combust from the heat given off by the flame. You must ensure that the fabric is well out of reach of your candles. Be creative.
6. Create a tent for your next backyard dinner party. Build a frame out of wood and cover it with sheer fabric to house your dining table. The four posts used to create your frame can be inserted into pots that have been filled with concrete, sand or dirt to ensure the frame stands upright. Once the frame has been completed and is standing upright you are ready to cover the frame with sheer fabric. Adorn the awning with beads, crystals, flowers or fruits.

7. Cover the poles of your tent with sheer gauze and flowers and greenery.
8. For an outdoor buffet create an awning that will cover the entire length of the buffet.
9. Set the stage for a romantic wedding ceremony. Create a small tent made from a wood frame that will stand upright at the altar where the ceremony is to be performed. The four poles of the frame can be inserted into large potted flower arrangements or pots of concrete to ensure that the tent stands upright. Cover the structure with sheer fabric that drapes down to the ground. In the top four corners of the tent place flowers and greenery draping them down the length of the wooden tent poles.
10. For a stunning party setting utilize a clear tent. There are party rental supply companies that have a myriad of tents to choose from.
11. Hang baskets of flowers from your tent ceiling.
12. Direct Gobos with various designs or the initials of the bride and groom at your tent ceiling.
13. Drape sheer fabric around tent columns. Hang tulips upside down around the tops of the columns.
14. Cover tent poles with curtains. Utilize colors that match your color scheme.
15. Set up a stage with a canopy for a four string quartet to be staged upon.
16. Hang sheer gauze swags that extend from the center point of a tent ceiling to the outside perimeter of the tent ceiling.
17. Create a canopy to cover a sweetheart table. Splash lighting in a pale color onto the sheer fabric of the canopy. Utilize chairs designed just for the bride and groom to give a feeling of royalty.
18. Hang chandeliers from the ceiling of your tent. Hang flowers from the chandelier as well as greenery and strands of crystals.
19. Create a canopy for the sweetheart table using a wood frame and cover it with sheer fabric. Hang flowers, crystals and candles from the frame of the canopy.
20. Utilize long tables for your dining arrangement. Create canopies to cover the tables using sheer fabric as the cover and decorate to embellish the design. This is great for a backyard dinner.
21. For a wedding reception by the pool create intimacy for the bride and groom by setting up a cabana near the pool. Place a sofa and table inside the cabana.
22. Utilize many cabanas around a pool and lounges for guests to relax upon.

BACKDROPS
Backdrops are just that. They are much like the painted canvas that drapes across the back of a stage except that these backdrops are not limited to canvas paintings.

1. For a wedding ceremony backdrop hang sheer fabric and arrange potted dry branches, flowers or potted plants in front of the fabric. Place lighting behind the fabric.
2. **TIP: Party rental supply companies have a myriad of backdrop designs to match any theme.**
3. Use fiber optics to create a backdrop with a starlit theme.
4. For a romantic backdrop hang a curtain of small white lights on the wall behind the wedding cake.
5. Hang sheer sparkling fabric on the walls of your dining area for an elegant look to a romantic dinner.
6. Create a florescent wall for a ceremony backdrop or as part of your decorating scheme.

7. TIP: To separate a wedding ceremony from a reception that will be held in the same space, utilize pipe and draping to create two separate areas.

8. Use willow branches to create a stunning backdrop for your wedding ceremony. Instead of creating an arch way with the branches place an arrangement of willow branches on each side of the altar. Decorate them with fresh flowers, lights or crystals.

9. For a decoration for the wedding altar place a square table on each side of it and sit flower arrangements or potted flowers on each table.

10. Have your wedding ceremony in front of a water fall.

11. Create a wall of twinkling lights as a backdrop for your wedding ceremony.

12. A lake complete with mountains makes a great backdrop for a wedding ceremony.

13. Create intimate spaces in your banquet room by hanging sheer fabrics, splashed with color created by light, in between your dinner tables.

14. Use four columns approximately 6-ft tall, three pieces of pine wood approximately (1"x2"x6'), two to four potted flower arrangements and glass votive candles to create a stunning backdrop. Evenly space the four columns in back of the altar where your ceremony is to be performed. Place the end of each pine wood board directly on top of each column so that they are connected. Place a potted plant on top of each column and arrange glass votive candles down the length of each pine wood board. You could use this idea as an entrance to a reception area as well.

15. For a beautiful backdrop at the altar, place three ficus trees on each side of the altar, insuring that the pots are covered with fabric. Hang crystals, swags of flowers and lights in the tree branches.

16. Another great backdrop for a ceremony or way to showcase the head table is to hang a sheer curtain with the names of the bride and groom attached in the back ground. Backlight the curtain after it has been hung.

17. Stage your wedding ceremony in front of an historic building or architectural beauty.

18. Use columns as an easy way to create a stunning backdrop for a wedding ceremony. Utilize 4-ft - 6-foot tall columns spaced evenly in a box design at the ceremony site. Place palm branches on the tops of the columns and potted flowers at the base of the columns. The minister, bride, groom and wedding party will all gather within this frame of love.

19. Showcase the bride and groom by setting up a small stage in the center of the banquet hall and place the bride's and groom's table on the stage. Decorate the stage with flowers or potted plants. Remember the bride and groom are the stars of the show.

20. Set up your ceremony around a garden fountain. Arrange seating to face the fountain and place the altar in front of the fountain.

21. For a beautiful ceremony backdrop hang swags of fabric from the ceiling and place a large vase of fresh cut flowers or potted plant beneath the swags.

13: THE AISLE

What is the Aisle and What to Do With It?

What can you say about the aisle? Actually there is plenty to say. The aisle according to the Webster's New Dictionary is the passage between sections of seats. At a wedding ceremony it is so much more. The aisle is the path leading to the altar. The wedding processional walks this path and resides at the altar anxiously awaiting the arrival of the bride. The groom waits at the altar for the bride to take her walk down the aisle. The father of the bride escorts the bride down this path to give his daughter in marriage. At this moment all eyes are on the bride.

There are many ways to dress up the aisle. It is customary to label sections of seating for the bride's family and guests as well as the groom's. Use aisle markers that are creative in design. Perhaps you could hang aisle markers that have a picture of the groom and a picture of the bride on each side. Maybe you want aisle markers that denote seating for the mother and father of the bride or other special guests.

You can purchase custom aisle runners or decorate the chairs that line the aisle. Search the internet for companies that sell wedding decorations or check with your florist. The florist can help with floral arrangements to decorate seating as well as supply petals to line the aisle. The list below gives some unique ideas for turning a plain aisle into a stunning aisle.

THE AISLE: 37 Ideas for Adorning Yours

1. Decorate the aisle to the wedding ceremony with iron rod candle holders designed for outdoor usage. Begin by placing a potted plant by each chair that lines the aisle. Use potted flowers or greenery. Use both by alternating pots of flowers and pots of greenery. Next insert an iron rod candle holder into each potted plant. Light the candles at the appropriate time.
2. Create a show stopping aisle at an outdoor wedding ceremony. To create this luminous aisle way to the altar utilize candles that hang from iron rod hooks that have been secured into the ground next to each chair that lines the aisle. Hang a candle and some flowers from the hook at the top of the rod.
3. For a romantic aisle to the wedding ceremony create a beautiful runner by using ribbons in colors to match your color scheme and basket weave the ribbons to make an aisle runner.
4. Decorate the aisle to the wedding ceremony by placing candelabras next to each chair that lines

the aisle. Decorate the candelabras with flowers and ribbons or ribbons strung with crystals. Light the candles at the appropriate time.

5. For a romantic wedding ceremony line the entire length of the aisle with a wire arch covering that has been decorated with flowers, grape vines and grapes or small white lights. Choose colored lights to match your color scheme to lighten up your arch covering.

6. Decorate your aisle to the altar with swags of sheer fabric. Create wire arches that will extend from the top edge of each chair that lines the aisle to the altar. Drape each wire arch with the sheer fabric. Add sparkle by wrapping strings of small white lights around each wire arch.

7. For a fall wedding ceremony scatter the aisle with multi-colored leaves.

8. For a beautiful aisle to the altar place a tall standing candle next to each chair that lines the aisle. Line the sides of the aisle with rose petals.

9. For a simple romantic way to decorate the aisle to the wedding altar scatter rose petals up and down.

10. A unique way to decorate your aisle with grace and beauty is to hang swags of sheer fabric from the ceiling of your wedding chapel so that they line the aisle from above.

11. Scatter rose petals on a stage set up for a wedding ceremony.

12. To create a stunning aisle create arches out of wire and flowers and attach them to the chairs that line the aisle. The arches will extend from the top outside corner of one chair to the next until you have attached wire arches to each chair that lines the aisle.

13. Utilize a customized aisle runner. Have a design or initials as part of your aisle runner.

14. To create a beautiful aisle and set the stage for a lovely ceremony line your aisle with pillar candles. Place a pillar candle next to each chair along side of the aisle. When you reach the first row of chairs create a circle with the candles that enrobes the ceremony area. Place a potted flower next to each pillar candle. Be sure to include potted flowers next to each pillar candle that encircles the ceremony area. The bride and groom will stand inside the circle so be sure to have a covered awning above the circle to protect the wedding party from bright sunlight or rain.

15. Have a white carpet runner for the aisle to the altar. Strew rose petals down the length of the runner.

16. Have sheer fabric swags extend from each chair that lines the aisle to the altar. Place a flower on each chair above the swag.

17. Lay a garland of flowers on the floor on each side of the aisle leading to the ceremony.

18. At the altar, place a monogram with the initials of the bride and groom on the floor.

19. Decorate the aisle to the altar with rose petals strewn in swirling patterns.

20. Decorate the aisle with rose petals creating the initials of the bride and groom on it or at the altar site.

21. Place columns strategically down the aisle and set flower arrangements on them.

22. Decorate with red and white rose petals. Create hearts out of red rose petals and lay white rose petals around the hearts.

23. Decorate with red rose petals creating hearts to line the aisle.

24. Another unique way to line your aisle is to place tall cylindrical vases next to each chair in each row that lines the aisle. Arrange orchids in the vase and fill with water. Place a round glass tray on top and place flower petals and candles in it.

25. **TIP: Use aisle markers, to denote where special guests, such as the mother and father of the bride will be sitting at the wedding ceremony.**
26. Use lighting to highlight the aisle.
27. Use lighting to highlight the aisle with the initials of the bride and groom or hearts.
28. For a unique path to the altar, place rose petals in ring designs down the length of the aisle.
29. For an inexpensive way to decorate the aisle to the altar place floor stickers with the initials of the bride and groom or sayings such as, "I LOVE YOU," "I DO" and "FOREVER YOURS" on the floor.
30. Petals are a great way to decorate the aisle. Here is another way to be creative with them. Use white petals to create a background on the aisle and then compose the initials of the bride and groom on top with red petals.
31. Use willow branches for aisle décor.
32. At the altar, create a heart design out of rose petals on the ground. The bride and groom will stand inside of the rose petal heart.
33. Place a fabric runner on the aisle way to the wedding ceremony. At the front of the aisle place the initials of the bride and groom and create a heart design around them out of rose petals.
34. Use ribbons or willow branches grouped together to section off areas of seating.
35. Place bowls of rose petals next to each row of chairs so that guests can throw rose petals at the happy couple as they ascend the aisle.
36. Use shepherds hooks to hang candles for decorating the aisle.
37. For a way to add whimsy to your aisle create a design utilizing red, pink and white rose petals by forming dots of different colors and sizes leading to the altar.

14: A MISCELLANY OF IDEAS

Hopefully you have found some wonderful ideas for decorating throughout this book. This section lists more decorating ideas and some ideas for party favors.

MISCELLANEOUS: 122 Ideas for Themes, Napkins, Honeymoon Suite, Garlands, Table Settings, Number Stands, Place Cards, Party Favors and Various Ideas

PHOTOGRAPHS

1. Purchase tiny picture frames and stands to use as place cards at each place setting at your dining table. Create cards with each guest's name on them and place a card inside of each frame. This is a great way to identify where each of your guests will be sitting at the table and also makes a great favor for your guests to take home with them at the end of the night.
2. Allow the guests to create images of magic moments at your reception. Have disposable cameras available for guests to take pictures. Leave the cameras with the bride to use at a later date to post wedding photos online or to make available by email to the wedding guests. Do the same for a wedding reception.
3. For an event celebrating a family member, friend or colleague place a framed picture along with biography on each table. This would be a great way to celebrate family members at a family reunion.
4. For a wedding reception display a picture of the bride in her gown at the reception hall entrance.
5. At the wedding reception display pictures of the bride and groom as children.
6. Place a variety of framed pictures of the bride and groom in the middle of each banquet table for guests to view and reminisce as they dine.
7. For the center of each of your dining tables place a photo of the guest of honor on a number stand and center the stand in the middle of your table.
8. Hang enlarged photographs of your guest of honor throughout your reception area.
9. For a great wedding favor place a mini photo album with a picture of the bride and groom on it at each place setting. Inscribe the album with the name of the wedding couple, day and date of the event.
10. For a great wedding favor stand a small framed photo of the bride and groom on the charger plate at each place setting.
11. For a memorable invitation have a photograph of the bride and groom on the invitation cover.
12. Create a tribute to a loved one by putting together a slide show of pictures for your guests to view.

EVENTS YOU DESIGN

13. Place a photograph on poster board cut to fit a number stand and print the table number on the side opposite of the photograph. For a wedding reception utilize a photograph of the bride and groom. For a child's birthday party utilize a picture of the birthday person. If your guests of honor are celebrating an anniversary utilize pictures taken from a recent vacation that commemorates their anniversary.
14. To create a keepsake for the bride and groom rent a portable photo booth to set up at your wedding reception. Display the photo booth in a prominent location and set up a table next to it to display an empty photo album and some ink pens or markers. Let guests take pictures of themselves to place in the photograph album and pen good wishes as well. Place a sign in front of the booth that you have decorated with hearts and photographs of the bride and groom. Put this message on the sign.

Get in booth
Take photos
Place one in book
Leave your wishes for Lila and Jamison
Enjoy the evening!

This is a great way to create memories that are priceless.

15. Create a tree out of dried branches to position on the table next to your photo booth. After a guest has taken their picture allow them to pen their good wishes and then hang the photographs on the tree. This will allow your guests to enjoy each other's photographs while taking their own pictures inside of the booth.
16. Display vintage props for a photo booth.
17. Utilize digital picture frames prominently displayed at your reception.
18. For your table menu create a sign with the menu on one side and a picture of the bride and groom on the other side.
19. Display vintage props and costumes for a photo booth. Guests can utilize them in their pictures.
20. Let your guests take digital photos of themselves and other guests to download to a future website or Facebook page.
21. Create a special place card holder for the bride and groom or guest of honor at your next event. Use a favorite photograph or create a bride and groom and place a photo of their face on each figure.

THEMES

1. For a movie theater themed party set up two large screens in two different corners of your room and play movies during your event. Rent a popcorn machine, Slushie maker and purchase concession style candies for your concession stand. Utilize movie posters as decorations for your event.
2. Serve hot dogs and other concession style foods.

3. Stage a screen and movie projector in the back yard for a party for the kids. Play scary movies for an older crowd or animations for younger children.

4. For a themed event have the staff assigned to your party dress in costume to fit the event's theme.

5. For an event that has wine as part of the theme place an empty wine bottle in the center of the table. Use the cork with a slit cut in the top of it to hold your table number.

6. Rent pinball machines and other arcade games for a children's party.

7. For an adult themed party rent equipment and staff for a casino party. Have a cocktail waitress serve drinks and servers to pass hors d'oeuvres.

8. **TIP: Christmas is a time for giving. For your next Christmas party have your guests bring gifts to donate to a less fortunate child.**

9. Create an international flair at your next dinner party using bright colors evocative of a Moroccan theme. Use a large coffee table for a dinner table. Purchase colorful string beads to hang from the ceiling around your coffee table. Use colorful pillows to sit on. Lay a table runner of vibrant colors across the length of the table. Use candles to help set the mood. Print a list on paper of a Moroccan *Mise en Place*. Frame this menu and place it on the dinner table. Check the internet for recipes of Moroccan dishes that have lots of flavor. Finish the mood by playing music of Moroccan heritage.

10. For a child's birthday party show videos of the child growing up. Be sure to add commentary.

11. For a Hollywood themed party hire actors that look like celebrities to hang around your party and mingle with the guests. Be sure that they take photographs with the guests and sign them as a remembrance of a fabulous event.

12. **TIP: Remember party rental supply companies rent all sorts of props that can make your party successful. From giant champagne glasses to antebellum style backdrops if you can imagine it they can probably supply it.**

13. Create an archway with balloons.

14. Create columns with balloons. There are companies that will fill the balloons with helium and create designs for your next event.

15. For a musical theme utilize old 45 records to create table centerpieces with floral arrangements.

16. Create art utilizing newspaper or wrapping paper and an inexpensive frame.

17. For a carnival themed event rent a cotton candy machine.

18. **TIP: Utilize curtains to separate sections of your room. Use tie backs to hold the curtains open when you are ready to have guest exit the reception area and enter the dining area.**

19. Release doves or butterflies at your wedding ceremony.

20. For a pool party place a pool poster in the bottom of your pool. This idea is great for a birthday party, corporate party and as a way of showcasing the guest of honor at your event. Contact Aqua Art Enterprises for more information on pool posters.

21. Create a theme such as "love through the ages" with characters such as Romeo and Juliet, Samson and Delilah, Anthony and Cleopatra.

22. Use your color scheme to create inexpensive art for your event. Paint a canvas with splashes of paint to mimic abstract art. Hang art throughout the venue and highlight each individual piece.

EVENTS YOU DESIGN

NAPKINS

1. Create an artichoke or pin wheel out of a napkin and place the napkin in the center of your tallboy table. Place a glass votive in the center of your artichoke or pin wheel. To learn more about napkin folding procedures go to the internet and Google napkin folding or purchase a book on the subject.

LETS CELEBRATE!

2. For your table setting utilize special napkin folds such as angle wings or bird of paradise.

3. Utilize cloth napkins that have two colors and fold them in an attractive design such as a standing fan fold or a carnation fold.

4. An attractive way to display programs on your dinner table is to fold your napkin in a cummberbund fold and insert the program inside placing each one in the center of each place setting.

5. Use a bishop fold at each place setting to create a place for a flower to rest. Lay the napkin flat and insert a flower into the folded napkin.

6. Create an envelope fold for each place setting. Lay the folded napkin on a charger plate and sit it in the middle of your place setting. Tuck a few flowers into the envelope fold.

7. Create a band out of construction paper to place around your napkin fold. Hand write or print in beautiful type the name of the bride and groom and date of the event on the band. Place the band around a square napkin fold and lay on top of a charger plate at each place setting. Check the internet for companies that can provide this service. You can also use ribbon to create the napkin ring.

8. Personalize your paper napkins for your wedding reception. Be creative and have a quote engraved on the cocktail napkins such as: **I LOVE YOU, SWEET ON MY LIPS, I DO, ALL YOU NEED IS LOVE** or NEW **BEGINNINGS.** Be sure to encapsulate the word LOVE in a heart. More words for your cocktail napkins: **CHEERS, JOY, SALUDO, BON APPÉTIT, ART DE VIVRE, JOIE DE VIVRE** and **CELEBRATE STYLE! TWO HEARTS ONE LOVE, MEMORIES THAT LAST A LIFETIME.**

9. Use decorative wide ribbon to tie a bow around your table napkins.

10. Utilize black tablecloths with white overlays and black napkins for each dining table to create a black tie affair. Fold the black napkins in a tux fold and lay one in the center of each place setting.

11. Alternate napkin folds using a white napkin folded into a tux design and a black napkin folded into a cummerbund. Place at each place setting.

12. Fold your napkins so that the program fits into the top of the fold and the name card fits into the bottom of the fold. You will have an envelope fold with an opening at the top and bottom to fit your program and name place cards.

13. Place an artichoke fold under your soup cup before placing it on the saucer for presentation.

HONEYMOON SUITE

1. For the honeymoon suite, decorate the bed, laying rose petals on top of the comforter.

2. Place a heart of rose petals on the honeymoon bed and a rose on each pillow.

3. Create a trail of roses that extends from the elevator to the entrance of the honeymoon suite. At the entrance to the suite create an outline of a heart with the rose petals.

4. Place a tray with chilled champagne and chocolate truffles next to the rose petal heart on the bed.

5. Strew rose petals from the entrance of the honeymoon suite to the bed.

GARLANDS

1. Hang garlands of hearts at the entrance to your reception hall.
2. Hang garlands of hearts over the dance floor.
3. Hang garlands of hearts over the sweetheart table.

TABLE SETTINGS

1. Utilize a variety of glassware on your dining table.
2. Use charger plates to add detail to your table setting. They frame the salad course. Be sure to remove them after the salad course is finished.
3. For your table place setting utilize a solid color charger plate and a dinner plate with a pattern on it such as flowers.
4. Utilize clear glass charger plates.
5. Frame copies of your menu and place them on each table.
6. Place a bottle of wine on each dinner table for the oldest lady at the table to take home.
7. Utilize name cards at the head table.
8. Be creative with the menu you lay in your place setting by putting the words "What's for Dinner?" across the top.

NUMBER STANDS, PLACE CARD and ESCORT CARDS
NOTE: A place card sits at the place setting allowing guests to know who will be sitting at that seat. An escort card is used to direct them to the table where they will be sitting.

1. Use a cork from a wine bottle to make a place card holder. Cut a slit in one end of the cork and slide the place card into the slit. Stand the cork at the top of each place setting.
2. Create your table number using a piece of rice paper which has been folded in half. The front half will have the table number inscribed upon it and the back half will have an explanation of all of the goodies placed on the table. If many of your guests are of different nationalities then inscribe your explanation in English as well as the language of the other nationality.
3. For an place card holder adhere the place card to glass grapes. Give the grape place card holder as a favor to your guests.
4. For an alternative to place cards above your place setting hang them from the backs of chairs with decorative ribbons.
5. For an alternative to an place card use a paper band designed to fit around your folded napkin and engraved with the names of each guest. Place the napkin and monogrammed band at the appropriate place setting.
6. For a unique way to display escort cards, hang wire, ribbon or strings from the ceiling, above the location of your registration table. Adhere the place cards to the wire utilizing plastic clips or stickers.

7. Utilize place cards at the head table.
8. Use a decorative picture frame as a number stand for your tables.
9. Place a picture of the bride and groom or guest of honor on the back of your table number.
10. Customize your table numbers by placing the names of the bride and groom, date of the event along with the table number. Use stock paper that has a design embellishing it.

PARTY FAVORS

1. Create a basket of goodies for the wedding couple to take when they depart for their honeymoon.
2. Create special badges for volunteers that help with your event.
3. Place your party favor inside of small beautifully decorated boxes for your guests to take home at the end of your event.
4. M&M's have personalized candies for you to serve at your event.
5. Create a CD with a compilation of your favorite music and label the CD with any pertinent information pertaining to your event or a photograph of the bride and groom. Your guests can take the CD home. Use the CD as a place card for your guests by placing the guests' names on the CD and standing it on a small plate stand at each place setting.
6. Utilize white wax bags filled with candies, nuts or cherries as favors for each of your guests to take home at the end of your event. Place a message on each bag.
7. Purchase glass votive holders that have been monogrammed with the guests' names on them.
8. Fill a sachet with mini candies. Use candies that reflect your nationality. Every culture has candies unique to that country.
9. Chiclets has monogrammed gum boxes with the bride's and groom's initials and wedding date.
10. Purchase individual mints with wrappers that have a tux or wedding dress theme on them.
11. Give a bottle of wine as a favor to take home after a wine tasting. Place a tag inscribed with the essential information of the party on the front of the bottle. Check the internet for companies that personalize wine bottles.
12. Design signs of various sizes for your wedding adding personal touches such as flowers, hearts, sayings or a picture of the bride and groom.
13. For a wedding have a banner created with the initials of the bride and groom on it to hang above the entrance way to the reception hall. Have relatives such as the bride's sister, nieces or a friend create the banner. This will make the banner more special.
14. Have the names of the bride and groom stamped on ribbon. Use the ribbon for decorating party favors or flower arrangements. Cut a large enough piece of the ribbon so that the names of the bride and groom are intact and adhere it to the top of a toothpick creating a flag to stick in the top of cupcakes. Also use the ribbon to tie off dinner napkins that have been folded.

VARIOUS IDEAS

1. **TIP: At your next event be sure to place a basket of toiletries on your bathroom counter top with items that your guests might need but not have on hand.**

2. Add sparkle to your water fountain by floating clear rubber rings or aqua lights in your fountain. These rings have a flashing light mechanism in the top portion of the ring enabling them to twinkle for hours while thrilling your guests.

3. Have a dollar dance to collect money for the bride and groom.

4. **TIP: To keep your tablecloths from being blown off of your tables at an outdoor function place rocks on the corners of each table. Buy plastic clips that are used to skirt tables or use clothes pins as a means of keeping tablecloths on tables.**

5. **TIP: If you are having a program at your event that requires the use of a screen, be sure to project your floor plan onto it while guests are entering the room so that they can find their table with ease. Often times tables are numbered for assigned seating but guests have trouble finding them without assistance.**

6. For a unique send off for the bride and groom create wands as an alternative to tossing rice at the happy couple as they depart the reception. Cover wands with shiny wrapping paper and adhere long strands of ribbon to the ends of the wand.

7. **TIP: Serve your guests breakfast in bed. For guests staying in the same hotel, have room service, deliver preordered breakfast to your guests. Bagels and lox are a traditional breakfast offering. A continental breakfast of pastries, coffee and juice is a delicious way to say good morning to family and friends.**

8. Use signs inscribed with messages as a way to cover any wall pictures, breaker box or other unsightly wall blemishes that appear at your venue site. For a wedding place initials of the bride and groom, words such as: **LOVE, DESTINY, DEVOTED, PASSION** and **RAPTUROUS** on your signs. Be sure to have a calligrapher inscribe your signs.

9. Purchase toilet paper that has hearts or the initials of the bride and groom inscribed on it.

10. For your next event create signs by placing letters cut out of newsprint or colored paper into glass picture frames. Words such as inspire, enjoy, music and create are perfect for a music themed party.

11. Create a stage that will extend over part of a swimming pool.

12. Place the initials of the bride and groom on to-go cups.

13. Use a company logo on to-go cups.

14. Signs are a great way to get the message across to your guests. Place them in decorative frames and hang them strategically for guests to view. Use sayings or quotes that go with your theme. Messages such as:

TOGETHER (HEART) FOREVER PAUL AND TERESA
SOMETHING OLD, SOMETHING NEW, SOMETHING BORROWED, SOMETHING BLUE

15. For an invitation utilize romantic words.

MY BOUNTY IS BOUNDLESS AS THE SEA,
MY LOVE AS DEEP: THE MORE I GIVE TO THEE
THE MORE I HAVE, FOR BOTH ARE INFINITE.
From *Romeo and Juliet*

16. This idea came from a wedding where the couple was going to move to Africa after their marriage had become official. They had a table set up at the entrance to their wedding reception in which they displayed various postcards that depicted their lives together and the place where they would be moving too. The guests would choose a postcard and pen their good wishes to the couple on it. These would later be mailed to the couple at their new home for them to read and reflect on the wonderful time they had at their wedding.

17. When you have your programs designed for your wedding reception personalize them as much as you can by placing details such as the names of the bride's and groom's parents and grandparents on them. Be sure that the names listed are of family members that are present at your ceremony unless you would like to make a tribute to a parent or grandparent that has passed away. Also include the names of your attendants. List the music that will be played during your ceremony for guests that might be interested. Give a special thanks to your family and friends to show them your gratitude.

Add the traditions of: something old, something new, something borrowed, something blue and a silver sixpence in her shoe by describing each item. For example, "something old," the bride's wedding band and engagement ring include jewels that her mother, Julia Jacobs, gave to her. Something new might include, her wedding dress is new. Something borrowed might be, the bride's antique lace handkerchief was borrowed from the groom's mother, Irene Lee. Both Mrs. Lee and Eryn Lee, the groom's sister, carried this hanky at their weddings. Something blue might be the shoes worn by the bride and a sixpence in her shoe could be a penny that her mother placed in her shoe when she got married. The bride is hoping for the same good luck that it brought to her parents for 35 years.

18. Hang a sign above the bride's and groom's table. Place the date and the name of the bride and groom.

19. For a waterside reception location place the dance floor on the waterfront.

20. At your next event have someone video tape your guests as they arrive. Let your guests give their well wishes to the guest of honor. Be sure to play the video during the reception.

21. Surprise the guest of honor at your next event by video taping guests, such as loved ones, that cannot be present at your party.

22. Have guests enter through an arch of drapery and crystals. Showcase the arch with dramatic lighting.

23. Use personalized decals, with romantic script to dress up your dance floor.

24. At the entrance to your wedding reception use a decal with the message, "All You Need is Love" in fancy script placed on the floor.

25. **TIP: Be sure guests know their way to the reception site and banquet room by strategically placing signs to guide them.**

26. Set up a dry ice machine near the dance floor. When the bride and groom take their first dance turn on the machine so that they look like they are dancing on a cloud.

LETS GET MARRIED!

CONCLUSION

What if you throw a party and nobody comes? Well this will never happen if you use my book to help you plan your next event. EVENTS YOU DESIGN was created to help you do just that, create working plans for event spaces. It is to be the inspiration to help you compose a sparkling celebration, one that your guests will talk about for a very long time and keep them waiting in anticipation for your next event. Whether you are choosing interesting colors, decorative elements, a seasonal menu, a formal or informal party I hope this book will touch your artistic side giving you a sense of uniqueness when designing your party. Start with the basics, outlined within, planning and organization and you can't go wrong. Commit everything to writing. To be successful is to be organized. Dare to dream and you can create whatever it is you conceive.

I hope my book has inspired you in your endeavors to design a spectacular event. Share the tantalizing ideas within with the people that will be responsible for the success of your celebration so that they will be better informed and able to make your event a successful one. Exhaust all of the decorating ideas in this book to find the ones that work for your celebration. Reserve some of these ideas for future events. Be sure to adapt the ideas to fit your budget. Remember these ideas are limited only to your imagination so be sure to adjust them to fit your needs.

Lastly, enjoy, enjoy planning your party. Planning is a large part of the fun. When the big day arrives you will be prepared, you will be stress free and you will know how enjoyable it is to plan your own party.

Saludo!

CONTRIBUTORS LIST

The following pages contain a directory of companies in the Nashville area that provide services for events. I would like to give special thanks to all of them as most of them have been involved in making the same events I have been involved with a success. You will see their spectacular work in the photographs contained throughout my book. All of the photographs are pictures I have taken.

CAKES

The Bake Shoppe
thebakeshoppe.net

Crumb de la Crumb
crumbdelacrumb.com

Dessert Designs
by Leland Riggan
www.dessertdesignbyleland.com

Dulce Desserts
www.dulcedesserts.com

The French Confection
frenchconfectioncakes.com

GiGi's Cupcakes
gigiscupcakes.com

The Painted Cupcake
thepaintedcupcake.com

Party Pops by Julie
partypopsbyjulie.com

Jay Qualls Celebrity
Cake Designs
jayquallsinc.com

Signature Cakes by Vicki
signaturecakesbyvicki.com
2 Chicks and Some Flour
flourchicks.com

CATERING

A Catered Affair
acateredaffair.net

A Dream Come True
Events and Catering
adctcatering.com

Once Upon a Time Catering
onceuponatimecatering.com

Cawthon's Caterer Incorporated
jacksbarbecue.com

The Chef and I Catering
thechefandicatering.com

Chef's Market
chefsmarket.com

Enchanted Events Catering
enchantedeventscatering.com

Tomkats Catering
tomkats.com

EVENT PLANNERS

A Delightful Day Event Planning
on facebook

Amos Events
AmosEvents.com

Angela Proffitt
angelaproffitt.com

Ashley's Bride Guide
ashelysbrideguide.com

Big Events, Inc
Malcom Greenwood
malcom@bigeventswedding.com

Ellen Hollis Events
ellenbaumhollis@comcast.net

Elizabeth James
elizabethjames@comcast.net

Elliot Events
elliotevents.com

Fete Nashville
fetenashville.com

Gage Events
GAGEevents.com

Music City Events

amusiccityevent.com
Nashville Event Space
nashvilleeventspace.com

Nashville Wedding Planners Group
nashvilleweddingplannersgroup.com

Schermerhorn Symphony Center
Event Manager
Hays McWhirter
hmcwhirter@nashvillesymphony.org

Schermerhorn Symphony Center Catering
and Events Sales Manager
Bruce Pittman
bpitman@nashvillesymphony.org

Signature Events Inc
SignatureEventsInc.net

Wedding 101
Nashville.wedding101.net

EVENT RENTALS
Accent Designs
accenttn.com

Fabu Event Rentals
fabueventdecor.com

Grand Central Party Rentals
grandcentralpartyrentals.com

FLORISTS
A Village of Flowers
avillageofflowers.net
Branches
branchesfloral.blogspot.com

Enchanted Florist, The
theenchantedfloristtn.com

Ilex for Flowers
www.facebook.com/IlexforFlowers

Melissa Marie Floral Design
melissamariefloraldesign.blogspot.com

OSHI
oshiflowers.com

The Tulip Tree
thetuliptreeinc.com

LIGHTING
Shermerhorn Symphony Center
Production Manager
Brian Doane
bdoane@nashvillesymphony.org

Nashville Event Lighting
Nashvilleeventlighting.com

MUSIC
Blue Tone Music
bluetonemusicusa.com
Craig Duncan Band
craigduncanmusic@bellsouth.net

I Do Music
idomusic.com

Gary Musick Productions
garymusick.com

The Jimmy Church Band
thejimmychurchband.com

Nashville Party Authority
NashvillePartyAuthority.com

Pat Patrick
www.patpatrickband.com

Tyrone Smith Revue
www.supert.com

PHOTOGRAPHERS
Ace Photobooths
acephotobooths.com

Jay Farrell Photography
jayfarrellphotography.com

Photo Booth Nashville
photoboothnashville.com

Rachael Moore Photography
Rachaelmoorephotography.com

RENTAL COMPANIES
BBJ Linens
bbjlinens.com

Classic Party Rentals
classicpartyrentals.com

Connie Duglin Linens
connieduglin.com

Events Plus
eventsplusnashville.com

Liberty Party Rental
libertypartyrental.com

Music City Tents and Events
musiccitytentsandevents.com

Southern Events
southerneventsonline.com

Visual Elements
veevents.com

VENUES
Schermerhorn Symphony Center
nashvillesymphony.org

INDEX

INDEX

GLOSSARY

accouterment or accoutrement: an accessory item of equipment or dress. Often used as plural.

amuse bouché: is a bite-sized piece of food. An amuse bouché spoon is similar to a soup spoon, upon which is served a tiny morsel of food. Amuse bouche: In French, "to amuse the mouth."

bakers fern: a common filler green used to adorn floral centerpieces and arrangements. Also known as leather leaf. Available thorough florists.

baron of beef: he term has come to refer to the large joint of beef that includes the loins and both legs. Baron of Beef is a British term and in the U.S. the designation means any cut of beef that is well suited to roasting or braising .

BEO: a banquet event order

bon appetit: in French is a toast meaning "good appetite."

bottle cozies: thermal wraps to go around soda and beer bottles to keep liquids cool.

bouillon: a clear liquid that is traditionally made by boiling meat, bones, and vegetables together.

bouquet garni: French term referring to carrots, celery and onions utilized to flavor stocks, soups and stews. They are placed in cheese cloth and tied off so that they may be removed after the cooking process has finished.

bundt pan: used to bake a **bundt cake,** shaping it into a distinctive ring shape.

butler pass: to have a server carry a tray of food (as in hors d'oeuvres or beverages) to offer guests during a reception.

charcuterie: is the branch of cooking devoted to prepared meat products, such s bacon, ham, sausage, terrines, *galantine* s, *pâtés* and *confit*, primarily from pork. Charcuterie is part of the *garde manger* chef's repertoire.

Cherry picking: removing a plate from the guest's place setting as each one finishes eating as opposed to clearing an entire table all at once.

chèvre: cheese made from goat's milk.

collins glass: a collins glass is a glass tumbler which typically contains 10 to 14 fluid ounces (300 to 410 ml) and is used to serve mixed drinks, especially Tom Collins cocktails. It is cylindrical in shape and narrower than a highball glass.

cloth: to throw a floor length tablecloth over a table and cover it so that the legs do not show.

color wheel: spectrum represented as a circular diagram showing colors as related to each other.

confit: 1: meat (as goose, duck, or pork) that has been cooked and preserved in its own fat. 2: garnish made usually from fruit or vegetables that are cooked until tender in a seasoned liquid.

coulis: a vegetable coulis is commonly used on meat and vegetable dishes, also as a base for soups or other sauces. Fruit coulis are most often used on desserts.

Couverture: chocolate, a very high quality chocolate of extra cocoa butter (32-39 percent).

crème brûlée: French, a Trinity cream dessert or custard dessert covered with caramelized sugar. [literally, "burnt cream"]

croquembouche: a tall cone-shaped cake or dessert constructed from balls of choux pastry filled with custard and coated with a hard caramel glaze.

crudités: small pieces of raw vegetables e.g. carrots and cucumbers, eaten as an appetizer or snack, often served with a dip.

deipnosophist: a person who is a master of dinner table conversation.

digestif: French, something, especially a drink, taken as an aid to digestion, before or after a meal.

faux pas: French, a social blunder.

framboise: French word for raspberry, and is often used to refer to alcohol distilled with the fruit.

French boned: To "french" a bone means to cut the meat away from the end of a rib or chop, so that part of the bone is exposed. This is done with racks of lamb, beef and pork for esthetic reasons.

French style table service: is an upscale service. The waiter typically has a fancy cart that carries different types of food for the guests to look over before they decide what they would like. Sometimes this is only done for appetizers or deserts, and sometimes it is done throughout the entire meal. At times they serve an eight-course meal this way.

friandises: a variety of small sweets, preserved fruits, etc., served as petits fours or desserts.

ganache: a rich icing made of chocolate and cream heated and stirred together, used also as a filling, as for cakes or pastry

garde manager: one in charge of cold food preparation.

glow stick: a self-contained, short-term light-source. The light cannot be turned off, and can be used only once.

hors d'oeuvre: an appetizer or canapé served with cocktails or before a meal. In French, "outside of the ordinary."

lamé: fabric with metallic strands.

leather leaf: a common filler green also known as bakers fern, available through florists.

Lexan: the brand name for polycarbonate sheet and resin in a wide range of grades. Used in banquet service to ice down beverages, containers are larger than a champagne bucket.

luge: An ice luge is a type of ice sculpture made from a large block of ice that has a narrow channel carved through where liquid is poured.

macedoine: a mixture of diced vegetables or fruit served as a salad.

mise en place: in French is the order of things as it pertains to food.

méthode champenoise: the traditional method used in the Champagne region of France to produce the sparkling wine known as Champagne. It used to be known as the méthode champenoise, but the Champagne producers have successfully lobbied the European Union to restrict that term to wines from their region.

mise en place: a French phrase which means "putting in place", as in set up. It refers to organizing and arranging the ingredients of a meal.

mousse: French for "foam." a prepared

food that incorporates air bubbles to give it a light and airy texture.

nonpareils: a decorative confectionary of tiny balls made with sugar and starch.

oasis: is a trademarked name for wet floral foam, the spongy phenolic foam used for real flower arranging. It soaks up water like a sponge and acts both as a preservative to prolong the life of the flowers and a support to hold them in place.

petit four: French, "small oven," a small confectionery eaten at the end of a meal with coffee or served as part of dessert.

paleta: a Latin American ice pop made from fresh fruit.

pommes frites: French term for french fries.

port: dessert wine fortified with brandy.

prosciutto: Italian term applied to all hams.

restaurant captain: also known as Chef de Rang, the captain is the position between headwaiter and the rest of the wait staff.

RSVP: in the context of social invitations, RSVP or Rsvp is a request for a response to an invitation. French: *répondez s'il vous plaît*, meaning "Please respond ."

roux: Equal parts butter to flour. Use 1 tablespoon of butter to 1 tablespoon of flour. The roux is used to thicken sauces, soups and gumbo.

sauté: to cook food quickly and lightly in a little butter, oil, or fat. You need really high heat. In French, "to jump."

sabayon: French, a dessert or sweet sauce made with egg yolks, sugar, and wine beaten together over heat till thick: served either hot or cold

Saludo: a Spanish toast meaning "greetings."

satay: also sa·té or sa·te, a dish of southeast Asia consisting of strips of marinated meat, poultry, or sea food grilled on skewers and dipped in peanut sauce.

seating styles: banquet style is where you have long tables connected together like the shape of an 'E'.

reception style is when there is one long table either at floor level or raised along one wall of the event area and the rest of the tables are round.

theater style seating is an arrangement of chairs in rows or arcs that all face the same point in the room. There are no tables or desks used in theater style seating. Some people may also call this cinema style seating.

shot glass is a small glass designed to hold or measure spirits or liquor, which is either drunk straight from the glass ("a shot") or poured into a cocktail.

scenario: to introduce yourself, partner to guests and give them a description of the menu.

sommelier: French - wine steward, a trained and knowledgeable wine professional, normally working in fine restaurants, who specializes in all aspects of wine service as well as wine and food pairing. The role is more specialized and informed than that of a wine waiter.

Sterno: ("Canned Heat") is a fuel made from denatured and jellied alcohol. It is designed to be burned directly from its can.

tapas: a wide variety of appetizers, or snacks, in Spanish cuisine.

tiramisu: a dessert of cake infused with a liquid such as coffee or rum, layered with a rich cheese filling, and topped with grated chocolate.

A truffle is one of a type of subterranean mushroom, or the fruiting body of such a mushroom. French gourmand Jean Anthelme Brillat-Savarin called them "the diamond of the kitchen".

tulle: a lightweight, very fine netting, which is often starched. It can be made of various fibers, including silk, nylon, and rayon.

Varilite: lighting in a room that changes color every 30 minutes.

Visio: brand name - Microsoft Office Visio is a diagramming and vector graphics application and is part of the Microsoft Office suite.

wait staff: waiting staff, wait staff, or wait-staff are those at a restaurant or bar attending customers.

SOURCES

All Events Advisor
alleventsadvisor.com

American Heritage Dictionary
New College Edition

www.drgourmet.com

easteuropeanfood.about.com

eHow.com

www.thefreedictionary.com

google.com

Merriam-Webster
Collegiate Dictionary
Tenth Edition

http://office.microsoft.com

Webster's Free Dictionary
www.merriam-webster.com

Wikipedia

NOTES

NOTES

NOTES

NOTES

Books are like angels moving between the living and the dead.

—Beatlick Joe Speer

Made in the USA
Charleston, SC
04 February 2014